THE SOLDIER'S WAR

BLITZ EDITIONS

Published by Blitz Editions
an imprint of Bookmart Ltd
Registered Number 2372865
Trading as Bookmart Ltd
Desford Road
Enderby
Leicester LE9 5AD

ISBN 1 85605 263 X

This material has previously appeared in *Witness to World War II.*

PICTURE CREDITS
The publisher would like to thank the following organisations for supplying photographs for use in this book.
Every effort has been made to contact the copyright holders for the pictures. In some cases they have been untraceable, for which we offer our apologies.

Imperial War Museum; Musee d'Histoire Contemporaine; US Marine Corp; US Coast Guard; US Library of Congress; US National Archives; US Army Photo Services; Smithsonian Institute; J Baker Collection; Ford Motor Co; Robert Hunt Library; Bundesarchiv; Bibliothek fur Zeitgeschichte; Public Records Office of Hong Kong; Kyodo News Services; Australian High Commission, London.

THE AUTHOR
Karen Farrington is a writer and former Fleet Street journalist who has specialised in the study of conflict throughout the 20th Century. In compiling Witness to World War II she has personally interviewed scores of veterans from around the world, obtaining a unique insight into the war through the eyes of the men on the front line. Among her previous books is 'Fated Destiny', an historical pot pourri of the curious, shocking and mysterious which includes accounts of some of the greatest military blunders in recent history. Karen Farrington is married with three children and lives in Exmoor, Devon.

This book was produced by Amazon Publishing Limited
Designed by Wilson Design Associates

Printed in the Czech Republic
51765

COVER PICTURE:
Battle for Guadalcanal, August 1942.
(Peter Newark's Military Pictures)

The Soldier's War

BLITZKRIEG!

With hindsight, it is easy to see how and why World War II erupted. Germany, embittered by the swingeing reparations imposed after its defeat in World War I, suffered appalling economic disaster. Its people soon grew weary of being forcibly reduced to Europe's poor relation.

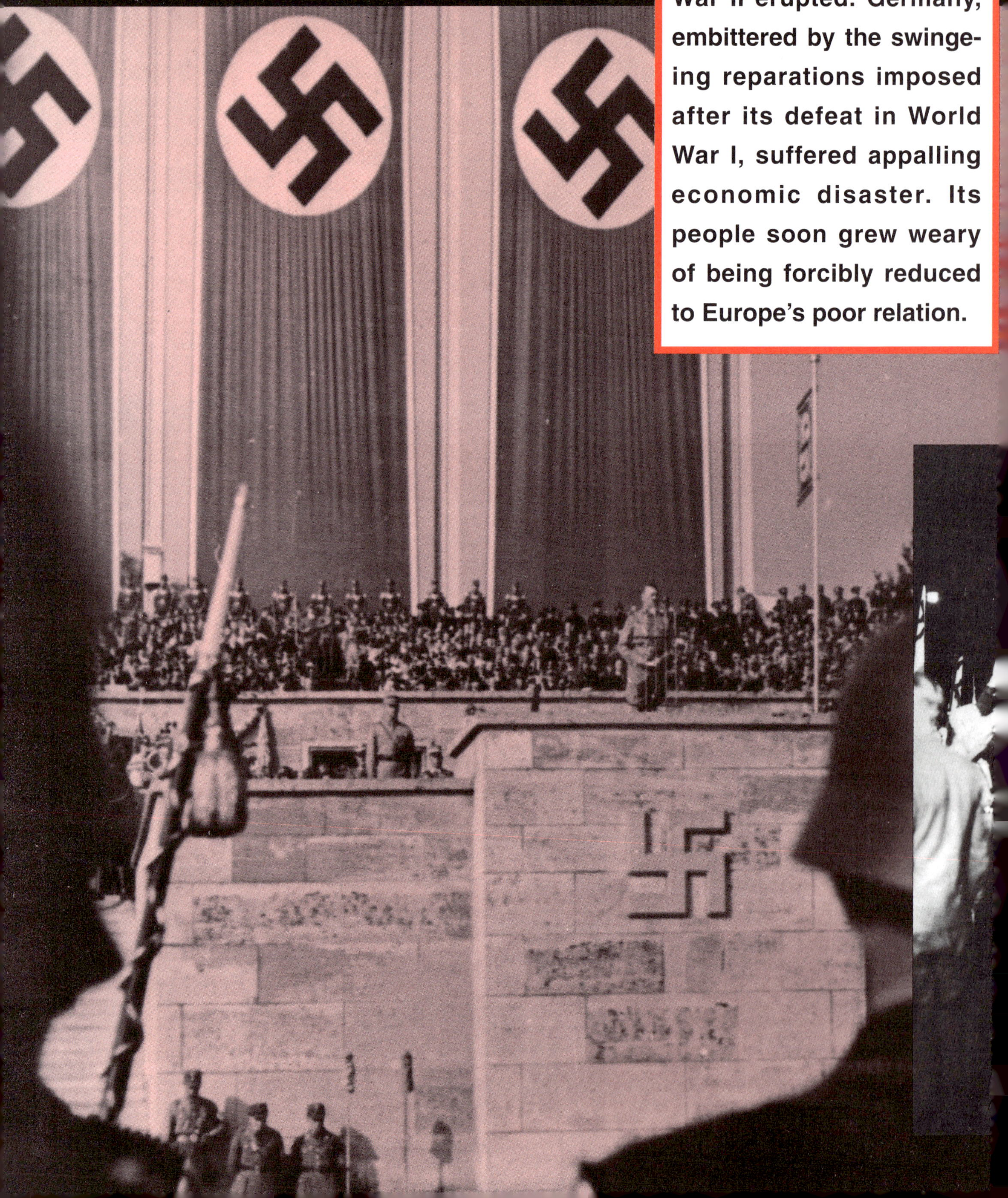

The time became ripe for a charismatic leader to sweep into power on the promise of returning Germany to its former glory. Unfortunately for the rest of Europe, those pledges for prosperity at home went hand in hand with an aggressive foreign policy. Nevertheless, Hitler offered the Germans an irresistible chance of stability, vitality and solidarity.

The only difficulty with which to wrestle is just how Britain and France missed the warning signs – and were catapulted into a war in September 1939 for which they were ill-prepared and poorly armed.

Both countries were weary of war, still reeling from the enormous loss of manpower and struggling following a deep world recession to remain on an even keel. At home they were far too preoccupied with domestic problems to heed the warnings of the few who witnessed what was really happening in Hitler's Germany. Violent anti-semitism was put down to the work of a few extremists. Many in power had a sneaking admiration for Hitler who achieved so much by cutting unemployment and building prestigious new 'autobahns'. His admirers conveniently overlooked the fact that Germany had concentration camps, no free press and no free parliament. And few outside the Reich had any idea of the military strength and firepower that the Führer was amassing.

When Hitler marched into the demilitarised Rhineland in 1936, many considered he was only taking back what rightfully belonged to Germany. The annexation of Austria in 1938 was looked upon virtually as an internal matter. Only with Hitler's demands for land from Czechoslovakia later that same year did Britain and France begin to sense the threat.

Hitler relished the chance to 'free' fellow Germans from 'Polish barbarism'

Their chosen path was appeasement, a negotiated agreement with Hitler designed to end his expansionism. When Hitler marched into Prague in the face of that agreement, Britain and France finally realised the folly of their actions.

All thoughts turned to Danzig, the free city in a Polish-held corridor which split Germany from East Prussia. It had long been a thorn in Hitler's side as he believed it was part of Germany. Hitler relished the chance to 'free' fellow Germans who he claimed were being subjected to Polish barbarism. There was considerably more trepidation in the minds of the Allies.

CARDBOARD TANKS

Much of Germany's rearmament had gone on covertly. Even when war broke out many British people were convinced that their former enemy, hampered by the treaty which ended the previous conflict, had tanks made of cardboard. Indeed, the Germans

Left: **A Nazi book-burning ceremony. Only works regarded as acceptable to the fascist dictatorship were tolerated.**

Far left: **Hitler addresses a Nazi party rally at Nuremberg in 1938.**

did carry out military manoeuvres with cardboard tanks back in the early 1920s before secretly importing and building their own real ones.

Meanwhile, France had the largest army and most impressive air force in the world. Most of its citizens prided themselves on the fact that Germany was unlikely to begin hostilities against such a superior force. As England viewed the Channel as an impregnable wall of defence, so France had the much-vaunted Maginot line. It took nine years to construct the frontier defences, brainchild of French minister André Maginot. The network of towers and tunnels was remarkable enough in itself. Had the Germans attacked it directly, it might have served its purpose well, albeit that it stretched only as far as the Belgian border, and not beyond it.

Hitler unleashed a new and frightening brand of warfare called 'Blitzkrieg'

This war, however, was going to be different to the first international conflict. Static trench warfare, which had claimed so many lives, was now an outdated concept – yet France and Britain didn't realise it. When Hitler invaded Poland in September 1939, he unleashed a new and frightening brand of warfare into the world – called 'Blitzkrieg'.

First to feel the heat of this 'lightning war', Poland lurched back in helpless horror when the German army crossed it borders at dawn on 1 September 1939. It took only a few hours for the invading force to quell

BRITAIN'S FASCIST LEADER

Oswald Mosley became the creator of the British Union of Fascists in the early 1930s after having been a member of both Conservative and Labour parties and having been linked for a while with the Liberals.

He had a lively, sharp mind and a clarity of vision. He was even branded the best political thinker of the age. But his frustration at the confines of the accepted political doctrines cast him to the margins where he hit upon the fascism sweeping Europe.

The British, however, were not entranced with uniforms and salutes in the same way as the Germans, Italians or Spanish, among whom fascism flourished. He became a figure of fun, never taken seriously even after the outbreak of war. He was nevertheless jailed in 1940 for four years. Following his release, he was vilified in Britain and finally moved with his wife Diana Mitford and two small sons to France. He continued to exercise his mind around political problems but failed to find a platform for his views. He died in 1980.

Left: **German soldiers survey the results of their fast-moving campaign in Poland.** *Top:* **Britain was braced for attack months before it actually came.**

Above: **Germany used its tanks to thrust ahead during the Blitzkrieg it unleashed with great success against Poland, France and the Low Countries.**

Polish defences. As the German troops and tanks rolled through the Polish countryside, the country's major cities were being bombed by the Luftwaffe and its ports were shelled by German ships.

Key to the success of Blitzkrieg was the use of tanks in large numbers and innovative style – they were still thought by Britain and France to be valid only as infantry support. The Panzer forces charged ahead independent of the troops, and wreaked havoc among defenders. Bursting through defensive lines, they harried the Poles from the rear, creating confusion and smashing supply lines.

The German air force had learned much aiding Franco during the Spanish Civil War, which ended in May 1939. Now pilots were putting this knowledge to good use and after a month Poland capitulated.

Above: **A French cottage is destroyed by advancing German troops, who put French and British defenders to flight.**

Poland's capital Warsaw held out for a few weeks longer than the rest of the country against the Third Reich. Heavy bombardment turned this once-grand city to rubble. As it surrendered, the Germans were triumphant. The hated Treaty of Versailles, which had condemned them to international servitude since 1919, was at last eradicated.

This time Britain and France refused to sit back and watch their ally being dismembered by Hitler. Both declared war on Germany almost immediately – although failed to do anything which would materially assist Poland – and braced themselves for the onslaught. Thankfully, it never came.

Despite the success of the Polish campaign, many German officers were concerned about taking on the might of the French army backed by Britain. Hitler was persuaded to abandon thoughts of an immediate push through the Low Countries into France, in favour of launching a spring campaign.

REALITY OF WAR

The reality of war was slow to strike home in Britain. When the feared air raids and gas attacks failed to materialise, there was an almost euphoric mood as people busied themselves sandbagging homes and putting up blackout screens in windows. The casualties in road traffic accidents caused by the rigorously enforced blackout far exceeded those caused in the war. Phrases full of mock indignation like 'put that light out' and 'don't you know there's a war on' typified the bureaucracy pervading the country. Joblessness stayed high, war production lamentably low. Reservists were being signed up for army duty surely but slowly, doing drills with bayonets and gas masks – and sometimes wooden 'rifles'.

Nearly 200,000 soldiers in the British Expeditionary Force were sent to France where they dug in on the Belgian border. By now, Germany had mobilised six million men.

Hitler was concerned at the ease with which the British navy had managed to raid a German ship in Norwegian waters. On 9 April 1940 his troops moved into Denmark and Norway in what promised to be another short, sharp campaign.

Denmark was without an army and acquiesced the following day.

Norway, deeply anti-militarist by tradition, nevertheless put up a fight despite the evident popularity with which the Germans were greeted in some quarters. Churchill himself was looking at the possibility of occupying Norway to reap the rewards of its strategic position. The government would do no more than lay mines in Norwegian waters to disrupt a vital German supply line. In fact, the Royal Navy was doing just that when some of the invasion force from Germany sailed up. There was a skirmish in which some damage was inflicted on German ships. That was the only glimmer of optimism in what turned into an otherwise disastrous escapade.

Churchill himself was looking at the possibility of occupying Norway

Britain sent landing parties to key points, hoping to steal a march on the Germans. But the small-scale campaign was ill-planned and improvised. The poorly equipped troops had no artillery and no air cover, whereas the Luftwaffe was in control of many Norwegian airstrips and was making full use of them. It wasn't long before the British, and the French forces with them, were forced to withdraw in disarray.

The debacle outraged many people and MPs in Britain, who feared the country was only making a half-hearted attempt at war. On 7 May there was a debate in the House of Commons in which Prime Minister Chamberlain made a statement on

◆ BLITZKRIEG IN THE WEST

From 14 May 1940, German Panzer forces bridged the River Meuse and poured into Belgium and northern France, driving all before them. The XIX Panzer Corps under Guderian crossed at Sedan, the XLI Panzer Corps (Reinhardt) at Monthermé, the XV Panzer Corps (Hoth) at Dinant, while Höpner's XVI Panzer Corps swept down from the north east. Within days, German tanks were at the Channel, but then paused. The British attempted a counter-attack at Arras, while the French planned a similar move from the south. These efforts came to little, however, and by the end of May, with German forces once again on the move, the British Expeditionary Force had its back to the sea at Dunkirk, awaiting rescue.

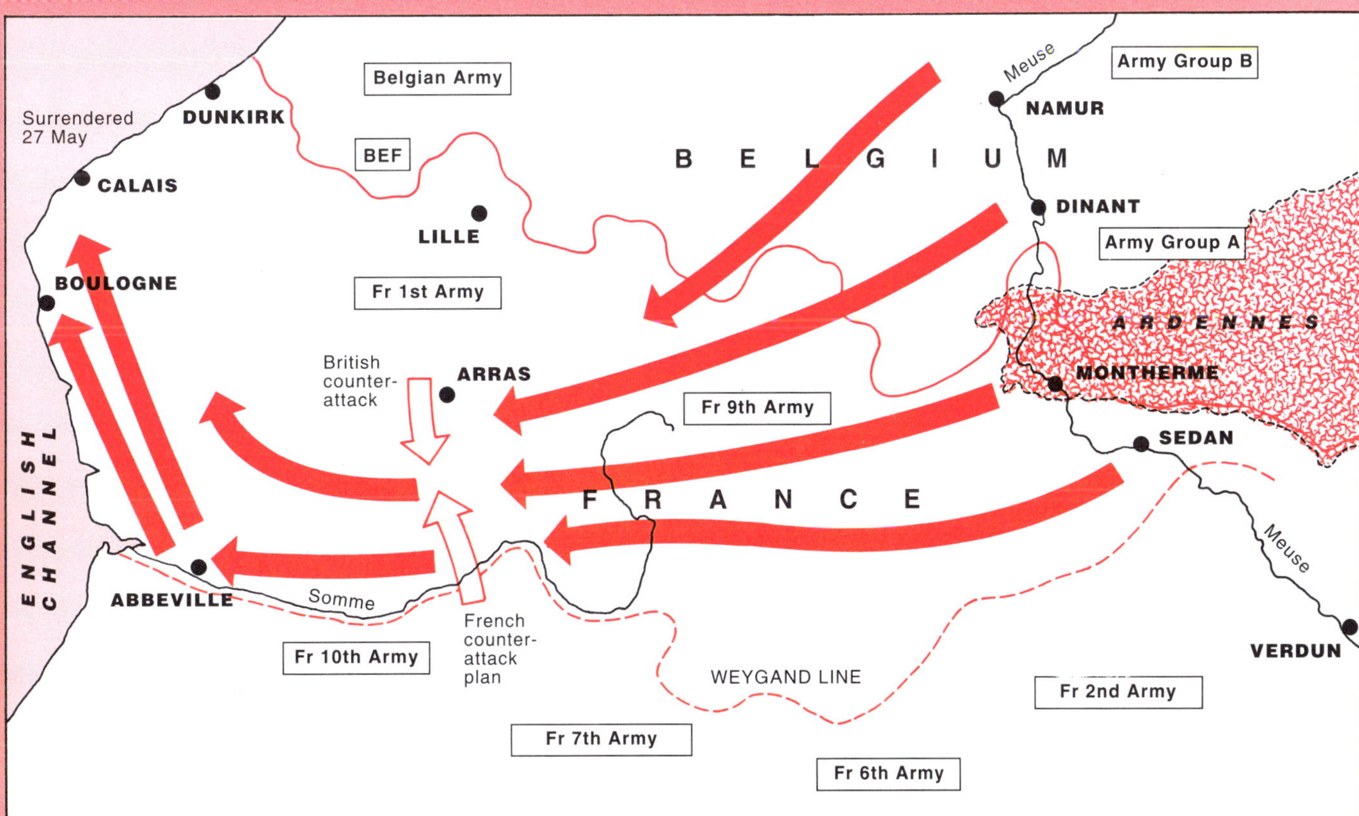

the Norwegian affair. The government won a vote of confidence by only 81 votes, too few for Chamberlain to continue.

The spring campaign got underway with a vengeance in western Europe

He resigned on 10 May, the same day that German troops made their first forays into Holland and Belgium. The spring campaign got underway with a vengeance as the horrors of Hitler's Blitzkrieg came to western Europe.

Airborne troops took the Belgian fortress of Eben Emael, chasing out the petrified defenders. At the same time in Rotterdam, 12 floatplanes landed on the River Maas. Out of each of them came an inflatable dinghy and a clutch of German troops ready to swarm over essential vantage points throughout the city.

HOLLAND FALLS

Also, there came the more orthodox methods of invasion, by Panzer forces over the borders. The French army and the British Expeditionary Force prepared themselves for a surge of German troops coming through northern Belgium. To their huge surprise, however, Panzer divisions had crossed the Ardennes, condemned as impassable by Allied commanders. Amid confusion, a division led by Rommel began a headlong rush west.

Holland capitulated on 14 May. It was another hammer-blow to the morale of the French. Without a dynamic leader – their commander in chief Gamelin was inaudible, indecisive and thought to be suffering

◆ EYE WITNESS ◆

Alf Turner joined a Territorial Army battalion in his home town of Barnstaple, North Devon, when he was 19.

In September 1940 we were stationed at Battle. Following Dunkirk it wasn't a case of "if the Germans invade", it was "when the Germans invade". So we had to put a minefield along the beach at Battle.

Not many people knew much about laying minefields. I was with a captain on the beach. We laid about four minefields and were starting on the fifth one. Our driver asked if he could help. The captain allowed him to lay a couple. The driver must have trodden on one and the explosion set lots of the mines off.

The captain and I were lucky to escape. A few days later our brigadier told us it was a vital area and asked us to go back to re-lay the minefield. I told the captain the chances of us coming out alive were only five per cent. Still, we had a job to do.

We re-laid about four and I was leading the way when the captain said he should go first. Soon after he took over he pointed to his right. In the middle of a crater lay the head of the dead driver. The shock must have unbalanced him.

Then the ground seemed to open up and I felt I was going into a great big pit. Yet actually I was being blown upwards. Our new driver was waiting on a shelf some 40 feet above the beach. He saw me go into the air above him and go back down again.

I was cross-eyed, had a perforated ear-drum and an injured arm. Still, I managed to get out of there. I was put under sedation for 24 hours, during which time I jumped out of bed three times. They even asked me to go down to the minefield again. I went – but this time they decided it was too dangerous to tackle again.

I was given a week's leave. The medical officer said if I had had any more, I wouldn't have come back. Going home in the blackout was hard. I had to race across pools of darkness, imagining all the time that parts of a body were coming out at me.

A fellow lance corporal blamed himself for the captain's death. He was a religious man and prayed very hard for me, knowing it was a dangerous job. But he didn't pray for the captain and he felt guilty about that.

Below: **Bewildered soldiers and frightened civilians roam the streets of Dunkirk as the Germans close in.**

Above: **Crammed onto the decks of a small steamer, weary troops of the BEF reach a British port.**

acutely from the ravages of venereal disease – the French army fell away, their lack of commitment a world away from the fighting spirit they showed so often during World War I.

The British forces found themselves racing back to the French coast, barely keeping a step ahead of the German advance. Despite an attempt to counter-attack at Arras in northern France, it soon became clear the situation was hopeless. Their commander, General Lord Gort, ordered his men to Dunkirk where they would await evacuation.

DUNKIRK

Luck was on their side. Hitler ordered his most advanced Panzer divisions to halt, wishing to conserve the cream of his troops for the invasion of Paris. It gave the British valuable time to install a defensive shell around Dunkirk – albeit fragile – behind which they could stage a daring, dangerous and vital evacuation.

Courageous rearguard campaigners held off the German advance while the Royal Navy sent in ship after ship to remove the stricken forces. By 31 May the news blackout on 'Operation Dynamo', the code name for the operation to save British servicemen, was lifted and scores of small boats set sail for France to give aid to the Royal Navy. Experienced mariners set off alongside weekend sailors to pluck as many men as they could from the beach. It was a tough voyage on small craft but each skipper was imbued with a grim determination.

Before the remaining defenders of Dunkirk surrendered on 4 June, 338,226 men – British, French and Belgian – had been carried back to safety. It was no mean feat, given that the official estimates for the evacuation were 45,000. Disastrously, most of Britain's armoury was left behind. There were too few guns remaining in Britain to arm the country's soldiers.

PARIS OCCUPIED

French soldiers, supported in the west by some British fighters, continued a disorderly retreat. Two weeks after Dunkirk, Paris was occupied and region after region continued to fall. When French prime minister Reynaud resigned on 16 June, his successor Marshal Pétain immediately sued for peace.

The final humiliation for France came on 21 June when Hitler had its leaders sign an armistice in the same railway coach where the German surrender was authorised following World War I. Now Britain stood alone against the might of the Third Reich with only 21 miles of English Channel to save it from invasion.

THE WAR IN AFRICA

When Italian dictator Mussolini dreamed of expanding his empire, he set his sights on Africa. Already the proud possessor of rich colonies, he yearned for more. Those held by the beleaguered British seemed to be ripe for the taking.

Far left: A British six-pounder gun comes under attack from long-range artillery.
Left: The Itaiian fascist dictator Benito Mussolini rallies his people.

Germany, which had been stripped of its African possessions at the end of the World War I, had no business on the continent. In any case, Hitler was preoccupied with conquering Russia. If the Axis powers had got their way, Italy would have swept through Africa and the oil-rich Middle East and Persian Gulf, kicked out the British and set up a vast empire while Germany concentrated on changing the face of Europe.

It was not to be. The Italians soon suffered a humiliating defeat at the hands of the British defenders of Egypt and were on the verge of being run into the sea when Hitler intervened. The Führer wanted Allied troops tied up in Africa, while he made progress with his plans elsewhere in the world. And he was mindful that whoever held North Africa had the key to the oil riches of the Middle East, a tempting trump card. He chose to take part in the North African conflict as a potentially profitable diversion.

So, in early 1941, the irrepressible General Erwin Rommel, who had been so successful in western Europe, was dispatched to save the Italians from annihilation, with the aim of securing a new front for the Third Reich. Rommel was a talented leader who prided himself on getting results. The British found him a surprising and bold adversary after the easy pickings of the Italians. But with the aid of troops from the Dominions, the British were determined to keep their vital foothold in Africa.

SEE-SAW WAR

It was the start of an indecisive see-saw war which lasted for three years and cost thousands of lives. Celebrated triumphs quickly turned to desert dust, as both sides discovered to their cost. British, Australian, New Zealand and South African soldiers got used to digging slit trenches in gritty, rock-hard ground,

Below: Thousands of Italian prisoners of war were taken as the British and Commonwealth troops made their initial push across the North African sands.

much as their predecessors had in World War I. Despite the best efforts of 'Desert Fox' Rommel and his men, it still ended with Mussolini's reputation as a war leader in tatters and dealt a death-blow to his regime.

Italy didn't declare war on Britain and France until June 1940 when Hitler's troops were at the gates of Paris and plans to invade Britain were already a reality.

The Italian strongholds in North Africa were Ethiopia – where Emperor Haile Selassie had been unseated four years previously – and Libya. In August Mussolini sent troops into British Somaliland in East Africa. With vastly superior numbers of troops, the colony fell to him within a fortnight. Bucked by their success, Italian troops stationed in Libya began to menace Egypt, in British hands.

Without paying heed to superstition, Italian forces crossed the border between the two countries on Friday 13 September and began a five-day advance which ended with them digging into their positions still some considerable distance from their goal.

OPERATION COMPASS

Egyptian ports became collection points for Commonwealth troops. British soldiers were joined by Australians, New Zealanders, Indians and South Africans for a mighty push against the Italians, code-named 'Operation Compass'.

On Monday 9 December British commander in chief General Sir Archibald Wavell signalled the start of the offensive. Before the week was out, 2,000 Italian prisoners were taken at Sidi Barrani. The Australian 6th Division took a further 30,000 prisoners when it overran Bardia on 5 January 1941.

The pattern was set. Sticking to the coast road, the Australians bagged another 27,000 prisoners on taking the strategically important port of Tobruk. Meanwhile, British troops dipped inland to by-pass a large mountain range.

By now the Allies were moving at a pelt across the Libyan region of Cyrenaica, capturing Derna, Beda

MONTY – DESERT MAGICIAN

Pride of Britain's armed forces, Bernard Law Montgomery, was born in London in 1887, although his ancestors were from Ulster. When he was two his father Henry was appointed Bishop of Tasmania. The island became his home until he reached his teenage years.

In later life, he often told how his childhood was an unhappy one. His mother Maud was strict and administered terrible beatings. He resented her greatly throughout his adult life.

After distinguishing himself as a soldier in World War I, it appeared he was married to the army. But to the surprise of all, in 1927 this difficult and irritable character married an artist and mother of two who had been widowed at Gallipoli. Warm and affectionate, they were a happy couple and had a son, David, in 1928.

In 1937, Betty died suddenly in a freak tragedy after being stung on the foot. Monty was desolate and threw himself once more into his profession. In the earliest days of World War II he led a division of the British Expeditionary Force in France.

Following the evacuation at Dunkirk, he was based in Britain until August 1942 when Prime Minister Winston Churchill made him head of the British 8th Army in North Africa. British troops, despite early successes, had been on the run from Rommel's Afrika Korps. It was Monty's job to turn the tide of the conflict – and it was one which he relished.

Just months after taking command of the Desert Rats, he scored a significant victory at the second Battle of El Alamein before chasing the German troops across North Africa into Tunisia where they finally surrendered in May 1943.

His next port of call was Sicily and he successfully led his forces up the foot of fascist Italy before being recalled to London. Before him was the most crucial command of his service life. Promoted to the rank of field-marshal, he was to help lead the Allied invasion of France. In charge of the key offensive was General Dwight D. Eisenhower with whom Monty clashed on many occasions. Later, Monty was criticised for his thoroughness. Accused of being too cautious, he frustrated his colleagues by refusing to commit his men to action until he was satisfied every small detail of the battle plan had been scrutinised and double-checked. However, his policy, which made for steady but slow progress, won the hearts and minds of his men.

Britain's hero soldier led the British and Canadian 21st Army Group across France, Belgium, The Netherlands and northern Germany to eventual victory.

After the war he held a series of high-ranking posts, including deputy commander of the North Atlantic Treaty Organisation. He was made a knight of the garter, and was created a viscount in 1946. He died in 1976, aged 88.

Fomm and finally, on 6 February 1941, Benghazi.

It was by any standards a whirlwind campaign. Allied troops travelled across 440 miles in just 60 days and dwarfed the Italian offensive which prompted the action. They were travelling across inhospitable terrain and even attacked Benghazi in a sandstorm. The retreating Italians who threw up token resistance were then caught in a masterful pincer movement by the British and Australian forces.

With Allied action against the Italians in Ethiopia making excellent progress too, Churchill must have revelled in the rout of the Duce. The British prime minister's satisfaction, however, was to be short-lived.

Churchill must have revelled in the rout of the Duce

Six days after the fall of Benghazi, Rommel arrived in Africa with his keen troops from the 5th Light Division and the 15th Panzer Division. He was welcomed by many resident Arabs who had long resented the British presence in North Africa. Within two weeks Rommel attacked El Agheila, the southernmost tip of the Allied gains.

Despite his lack of experience in desert warfare and a recurring mystery stomach complaint, Rommel was soon making big gains, sending a depleted and weary Western Desert Force back from whence it came. He excelled in warfare on the hoof and preferred a fluid campaign in which

◆ EYE WITNESS ◆

Bill Jenkins, a sergeant in the Australian infantry throughout the war, explains why so many Australians were keen to fight the Allied corner.

"At the time we had a population of seven million. We recruited in the first six months of the war over 200,000 volunteers. During the whole of the war, 750,000 people were involved. So percentage-wise I think we did reasonably well for the mother country. The old Australians were very much involved in Empire and considered a trip to England as "going home" even if they were not even born there. World War I was still in our memory, too. We were going off to finish the job that the soldiers then had started. There was the adventurous spirit, the deep feelings of patriotism that ran through many of us. And most Australians love a fight!"

GOLDEN

News Chronicle

SATURDAY, FEBRUARY 8, 1941 · RADIO PAGE 3 · ONE PENNY

No. 29,566

Haig

THE WHIRLWIND TRIUMPH OF BENGHAZI

Italians Caught on Two Sides by Brilliant Pincer Move

From BERTHA GASTER
News Chronicle Correspondent

CAIRO, Friday.

IN A SEVEN-DAY WHIRLWIND CAMPAIGN, THE IMPERIAL ARMY OF THE NILE HAS SWEPT THROUGH THE 175-MILE STRETCH OF HILL AND DALE OF CENTRAL CYRENAICA, SHOT PAST VILLAGES AND SETTLEMENTS IN ENDLESS SUCCESSION, SMASHED ENEMY AERODROMES IN A SERIES OF DEVASTATING RAIDS, AND TAKEN BENGHAZI.

Despite the broken morale of the Italians and the lack of any effective air opposition, the rapidity of the latest success is greater than anyone dreamed.

It was expected that progress over the plateau, where the country is eminently suitable for defensive fighting, would be slow and protracted. In fact, the rate of advance has been about as quick as troops could make it on ordinary line march without opposition.

On Thursday night our planes were still bombing Benghazi and the neighbouring aerodrome of Benina. Today both are in our hands, and the occupation of one-third of Libya is complete.

It is 60 days since the campaign against Sidi Barrani began. In that time we have advanced 440 miles from Mersa Matruh over hitherto impregnable desert, captured three well-defended strongholds, taken more than 110,000 prisoners, and brought Mussolini's North African Empire crashing about his ears.

Italian Prisoners For the Land

"I hope to get several thousand Italian prisoners of war to work on the land in gangs," Mr. R. H. Hudson, Minister of Agriculture, told farmers at Devizes.

Churchill to Broadcast Tomorrow Night

The Prime Minister, it was announced last night, will speak at 9 p.m. in the Home and Overseas Services.

Weygand Says: We Keep Bizerta

GEN. WEYGAND broadcast from Algiers yesterday a denial of reports that France would permit Germany to use Bizerta, base in Tunisia, with a view to eventual action in Libya.

Milch Warns Germany

"DANGER hovers over everybody in Germany," declared Milch, Field-Marshal Goering's deputy, last night in a broadcast from all German stations.

Hitler Reported In Vichy

From Our Own Correspondent

Invasion Ports Battered Again

From Our Own Correspondent

DOVER, Friday

LATE N

Death Sente

"Brave Engl

Here is part of the booty which fell into British hands at Tobruk. Line after line of Italian mechanised transport

Above right: **Australians march ashore at Suez in May 1940.**

Right: **The capture of Benghazi was an important first victory.**

Left: **Tobruk was a vital port which Rommel fought hard to win. But the besieged Australian forces held fast despite terrible hardships.**

he was ever ready to improvise. Unpredictable, incisive and single-minded, Rommel, rarely seen without his goggles, was an inspiration to the men of his Afrika Korps. Contrary to common belief, they were not specially trained for the tropics but underwent only a standard medical. Like their leader, they were professional soldiers who earned the respect of their enemy during the North African campaigns.

TOBRUK BESIEGED

Churchill had risked British, Australian and New Zealand troops from North Africa for the tandem campaign in Greece. It meant Wavell had been unable to crown his glorious advance by taking Tripoli. Now the Allies were paying for this.

By 3 April 1941, Benghazi had fallen once again. Soon Tobruk was under siege. The town was manned by a stoic Australian division integrated with straggling British and Indian troops that had become split from their units in the overwhelming German advance.

Australian commander Major-General Leslie Morshead organised sturdy defences around the town, installing every bit of artillery he could lay his hands on in the fortifications once held by the Italians. The bombardment from Tobruk took its toll on the attacking German and Italian forces. Rommel was by now far from his Tripoli supply base with its crucial stocks of water, food, fuel and ammunition. He needed the port as an alternative. The Australians, deeply entrenched, held fast. If Rommel made mistakes, it was here when his hand was forced by the gutsy Australians. His efforts to capture Tobruk cost him dearly.

Britain was able to receive new supplies from a Mediterranean convoy which delivered to Alexandria in Egypt. Tobruk was given support from the Royal Navy and the efficient Desert Air Force. Wavell launched a counter-offensive known as 'Operation Battleaxe' to relieve Tobruk overland. His golden touch deserted him, however, and thanks to the wit of his opponent it failed.

◆ EYE WITNESS ◆

Arthur Stephenson, of the Royal Artillery, was 21 when he joined up in 1939. He served in Africa and Normandy.

"I've got a lighter at home with a Canadian badge on it. In the desert I was trying to light my pipe. This Canadian came up and went to light it for me.

He was there one minute and gone the next. A shell-burst killed him outright. All that was left was his lighter. He was only three yards away from me and I was completely unscathed."

Rommel, who earned his 'Desert Fox' nickname through his cunning, now lured the British forward

Rommel, who earned his 'Desert Fox' nickname through his cunning, now lured the British forward by feigning retreat. When the armoured units came within range, the superior German anti-tank guns opened fire causing devastation.

It was a costly lesson to the British and one which lost Wavell his job. In his place came General Sir Claude Auchinleck, who arrived to find a stalemate as both sides sought to rearm. He orchestrated 'Operation Crusader' in November, once again with the aim of relieving Tobruk. During the eight months they spent holed up in the port, the Australians had not been idle. They delivered some severe blows to Rommel from their fortress, targeting tanks in particular. Now Auchinleck found a corridor for Allied forces to link up by December. Once again, however, victory hung in the balance.

Both sides benefited from aerial support. The Luftwaffe had easy access to North Africa from its bases in southern Italy while the RAF Desert Air Force proved crucial to the success of Allied troops on the ground. Rommel had recharged his men and was looking for revenge. He beat Auchinleck to a counter-attack which he made as early as January 1942 and forced the Allies back once more. There followed a fierce exchange in May at Gazala in which the bold Rommel led a charge through enemy minefields and lines. Auchinleck was squeezed out of Libya, back into Egypt. The retreat was compounded when Tobruk was surrendered in June by the South African garrison then holding it, after only a week under seige, and 25,000 prisoners were taken. Now Rommel was promoted to the rank of field-marshal by a delighted Hitler. Without pausing to celebrate, he pressed ahead with his campaign.

From decoded intercepted messages from Rommel, Churchill believed the German commander was in dire need of assistance

Churchill was devastated by the Allied armies' swift reversal of fortunes. From decoded intercepted messages from Rommel to Berlin, he believed the enigmatic German commander was in dire need of assistance and on the verge of capitulation. Churchill failed to understand that this sob story was a device used by Rommel to win more supplies and men – which were rarely forthcoming.

Rommel's men were, however, weary. Auchinleck's air and artillery bombardment as they advanced towards El Alamein had the desired effect and stopped them in their tracks. A brigade from the 9th Australian Division broke out of El Alamein and swept forward. But the efforts of the Australians and the 8th Army failed to do much more than dent the Afrika Korps.

Now it was Auchinleck's turn to feel the wrath of the British prime minister. While defending El Alamein in Egypt, he was replaced by General Bernard Montgomery.

Although painstakingly calculating and methodical, Montgomery had

Below: **Sir Claude Auchinleck served in Norway and India before succeeding Wavell in North Africa. But his failure to hold Rommel cost him his job.**

the same fire for victory inside him that drove his rival Rommel. With an injection of powerful Sherman tanks from America, Monty regrouped his British, Australian and New Zealand forces after fending off an unsuccessful stab at the defensive lines by the overstretched Germans in September and prepared his battle plan.

Monty preferred a confrontation rather than the more fashionable lightning manoeuvres perfected by the Germans. It was his aim to destroy as much of the enemy army and artillery as possible. In his words, it would be a 'dog-fight' and by his standards it was an almost reckless campaign in its intensity.

Arguably still medically unfit for command, Rommel found himself overwhelmed

The second Battle of El Alamein began on 23 October, the day Rommel returned to his post after a spell of sick leave in Germany to relieve his replacement who had suffered a heart attack. Arguably still medically unfit for command, Rommel found himself overwhelmed by the reinforced Allied army which for the first time now substantially outnumbered his own. He soon discovered that, even if he had wanted to, he was unable to adhere to Hitler's orders not to retreat.

Allied firepower rained down on the Afrika Korps. In fact, there was some disarray in Allied lines and the thrust forward was belated. But finally a bold brigade of Australians drove north, at immense cost in terms of personnel.

Montgomery regrouped and came forward again in 'Operation Super-

◆ EYE WITNESS ◆

Stanislaw Lachoda was an 18-year-old signalman in the 2nd Battalion of the Polish Carpathian Brigade, a volunteer group made up of Poles who had escaped Nazi and Soviet occupation. In August 1941 the brigade was taken from Alexandria to Tobruk by the Royal Navy to replace Australian troops at Tobruk.

Soon after 'Operation Crusader' got underway, I was seconded with two other signalmen for an operation to mislead and disorientate the enemy in the western sector.

Well armed with Brens, Tommy guns and a plethora of hand grenades, attacking squads wearing desert boots and overalls silently crept behind the Italian positions and, on a given signal, let everything go at the enemy.

It was only when the mission was accomplished that the Italians recovered from the shock of being fired on from the rear and it was then their turn to lay a heavy barrage of machine-gun and artillery fire on us retreating along the narrow wadi towards the safety of our own positions. Despite the failure of communication due to the destruction of our radio's antenna, our own artillery laid protective fire for us at the right time when we were clear of the enemy's positions.

In situations as fluid as desert mirages, those who dared and took risks were the gainers and the timid ones got what they deserved.

By 8 December neither side scored a resounding victory despite heavy human and material losses but there appeared signs that the battle-weary Afrika Korps was contemplating disengagement. Our own patrols confirmed that the western sector based on the hill Ras El Medauar was still held by Italians. It was our next target.

The attack on the southern slope of the hill was spearheaded by 2nd company to which I was attached as one of the signal patrol. Our job was to provide telephone links with the battalion HQ. We moved silently step by step through the treacherous minefields, along a cleared narrow lane marked by white tape.

There was chaotic fire from Italian Breda guns as well as flares as we edged along. The last obstacle, a thick concertina of barbed wire, was dealt with and a final jump into noisy heaps of empty tin cans covering the slope led us into an elaborate system of concrete pill-boxes and bunkers. Most of the Italians surrendered after token resistance, the stubborn ones were dragged out from murky and smelly hideouts. Before sunrise the white and red Polish flag was hoisted up. The capture of Ras El Medauar was celebrated with fireworks, using up a huge stock of captured flares.

charge', with New Zealand and British infantry going into the jaws of battle under cover of artillery fire. Rommel, who had been ordered not to retreat, replied in kind. But while the British had healthy supplies of arms and men, Rommel was far from his base. The creeping successes of Allied troops forced his hand.

ROMMEL ON THE RUN

Rommel's army fled back along the coast road, the scene of so many retreating marches, with Monty's 8th Army and the 2nd New Zealand Division led by the courageous and skilled General Freyberg at its heels. The Desert Air Force inflicted terrible damage. Monty refrained from attempting to outflank his enemy, guessing that British troops would not carry out this by-now familiar German tactic so ably. He favoured a set-piece move against Rommel and his confidence in old-fashioned text-book battlecraft paid dividends. There was another factor for him to consider, too. In November combined Anglo-American forces began landing in North Africa in the territory of Vichy France. These were the 'Torch' landings, the first slice of action seen by many American soldiers and British reserves.

While Vichy rulers were implacably opposed to Britain, their attitude towards the Americans was ambivalent. The local Vichy commander was persuaded to switch sides from Germany to the Allies in November 1942 after some skirmishes in which the Allies easily managed to gain the upper hand. This left the path clear for the fresh forces to take on the cornered German Afrika Korps.

Hitler in turn provided reinforcements at last, bolstering the defences of Vichy-held Tunisia where Rommel headed from Libya. He was not ready to seize an opportunity for a counter-attack. His troops were short on supplies and still in the minority. Despite the excellent defensive position offered by the mountainous borders of Tunisia, he realised the situation was hopeless.

AXIS SURRENDER

Rommel was recalled in March 1943. His men continued the fight until May when Tunis fell. The surrender of the Axis forces in North Africa came on 13 May, with the capture of 275,000 soldiers. It was a relief to the Allied army, which had by now known the very worst of desert warfare. Montgomery was hailed a national hero, and Rommel, although the loser, was in turn hailed a military master.

Left: **A pensive Monty displays his famed taste for unconventional battledress.**

Below: **American troops stride ashore unopposed during the 'Torch' landings, November 1942. They soon met fierce German defenders.**

BARBAROSSA – TARGET RUSSIA

Hitler has become infamous in history for his hatred of Jews. Yet he also singled out the Russians as a worthless, reviled race: he called them 'sub-humans'. It became his avowed aim to see the people in chains and Communism eradicated once and for all.

Before the war between Hitler's Germany and Stalin's USSR began, the German Führer laid down the ground rules to his generals. In essence, there were none:

'The war against Russia will be such that it cannot be conducted in a knightly fashion. The struggle is one of ideologies and racial differences and will have to be conducted with unprecedented, unmerciful and unrelenting harshness. The commissars are the bearers of ideologies directly opposed to National Socialism. Therefore the commissars will be liquidated. German soldiers guilty of breaking international law . . . will be excused. Russia has not participated in the Hague Convention and therefore has no rights under it.'

These words set the tone for a brutal and bloody conflict, far exceeding the ruthlessness shown so far by invading Nazi forces in western Europe.

Hitler's first problem, however, was how to bring the Russian Bear to battle at all. For months during 1939 the USSR's tyrant leader Stalin had been courted by Britain and France, both anxious to get Soviet support for the forthcoming hostilities with Germany. Hitler's disparaging views of Russia were well known, not least among the Soviet people themselves. In the circumstances, it seemed Stalin was a natural ally of Britain and France.

Left: Joseph Stalin. Hitler feared and detested Communism and all other left-wing ideologies. Stalin's regime in the USSR embodied all that Nazism opposed.

Above right: **'Barbarossa' unleashed the fury of Germany's erstwhile ally.** ***Below:*** **Hitler and Soviet foreign minister Molotov (left) reach an uneasy peace, 1939.**

FRAGILE PACT

Suddenly, however, the carefully wrought diplomacy collapsed like a house of cards. Out of the blue came the Berlin-Moscow Non-Aggression Pact, signed at the Kremlin by Ribbentrop, for Hitler, and Molotov, for Stalin, in August 1939. Hitler found himself the closest ally of his hated adversary. Stalin guessed it would at least buy him time before his country became involved in a war it neither wanted nor could afford.

'The war against Russia... cannot be conducted in a knightly fashion'

And the reason behind the gleam in Stalin's eyes at the signing of the pact was revealed just a month later. Two weeks after German forces marched into Poland, Russian forces invaded from the east. The two countries proceeded to partition the helpless Poland as they pleased. If Stalin was concerned that he was dancing with the Devil, he comforted himself that Britain and France would tie up sufficient numbers of German troops on the Western front to make the opening of a second front an act of idiocy by Hitler.

In November, encouraged by his easy success, Stalin engineered a war with Finland. When the Finns flatly refused to hand over disputed territory, the Red Army marched in, anticipating another quick victory.

Six weeks later their hopes had been dashed. The vastly outnumbered Finns put up a fierce fight, using superior tactics and winning some impressive victories. It wasn't until March 1940 that the war was finally over with the surrender of little Finland, time enough for the Finns to have inflicted humiliation on their giant neighbour, which lost an estimated one million fighting men. Hitler noted the failings and flailings of the Red Army with more than a passing interest.

Stalin was livid with the poor performance of his army. But there was no one to blame but himself for the debacle – as he had ordered the deaths of many of his leading commanders during a devastating purge of the army which began in 1937. It happened after whispers of a military uprising against him. Whether the threat was imagined or real, no one can say. What is certain is that Stalin wreaked a terrible revenge to defend his lordly position.

Stalin wreaked a terrible revenge to defend his lordly position

By the end of 1938 three out of every five of the Red Army's marshals were dead as well as 13 out of 15 army commanders. More than a quarter of the army's brigadiers and more than half of the divisional commanders had been executed, too. There was also bloodletting among the politicos involved with defence. Those that remained were untalented and uninspiring. They hampered the progress of the fighting force with

Below: **General Heinz Guderian, architect of Blitzkreig in the west, keeping up morale in Russia in 1941.**

outdated ideas, which included the abandonment of automatic weapons and the halting of the comprehensive tank programme in favour of horse-drawn artillery. So the army was left woefully lacking in experience, for which it paid a terrible penalty.

Nevertheless it was still the largest army in the world, although Hitler had other considerations than this in preparing his battle plan.

GREEK DIVERSION

By 1941 he was convinced he could overwhelm the Soviet Union and kill off Communism there for good. But he was compelled to delay the invasion due to the German involvement in Greece, an unexpected diversion which cost the Reich valuable men and time.

It was a late spring that year, too, leaving roads clogged with mud and rivers swollen by the slow thaw. Germany needed the best possible weather to make a clean, quick strike into the heart of its foe.

By the beginning of June, all the indications were that Hitler was ready to pounce. As many as 76 different warnings came to Stalin to that effect. Churchill gleaned top secret information from his Ultra decodes, telling of the proposed invasion. Spies stationed around the Axis world delivered similar warnings. One German soldier, a closet Communist, even escaped across the border to warn Stalin of the impending attack.

Still the inscrutable leader refused to believe Hitler would wage war on him. He remained primarily concerned about his frontier with Japan, the growing menace in the east. Even the rapid and unexpected fall of France failed to persuade him that Russia would be next on the German Führer's hit list.

Stubbornly, Stalin dismissed the international warnings sent to Moscow as scandalous rumour-mongering and barred his top army commanders from mounting defences along the border, for fear of provoking Hitler. He even had the runaway German soldier shot.

His policy of appeasement designed to keep Russia out of the war stretched as far as sending train loads of oil, grain and metals to the Third Reich even while its troops were congregating on the borders.

On 22 June he was forced to think differently. 'Operation Barbarossa' got underway with 165 divisions

Left: **The summer offensive against Russia progressed rapidly at first, until the German invaders ran out of good weather.**

Below: **A Red Army observer on the lookout for enemy aircraft in Moscow, 1941. The Soviets were ill-prepared for a German attack.**

THE GREAT DEBATE

By 1940, America was caught up in 'The Great Debate', about whether or not it should enter the war.

The largest body of isolationists campaigning to keep America out of the conflict was the America First Committee, centred in the Mid-West where anti-British and pro-German sentiments were strongest. Fascists united with Communists and radical Irish Americans in wanting to keep America neutral. In opposition was the Committee to Defend America by Aiding the Allies, founded in May 1940.

Among those contributing to the debate was Colonel Charles A. Lindbergh, who in 1927 became the first aviator to cross the Atlantic non-stop, and whose two-year-old son was kidnapped and murdered in 1932. He had visited Nazi Germany, inspected the Luftwaffe and declared the force was invincible.

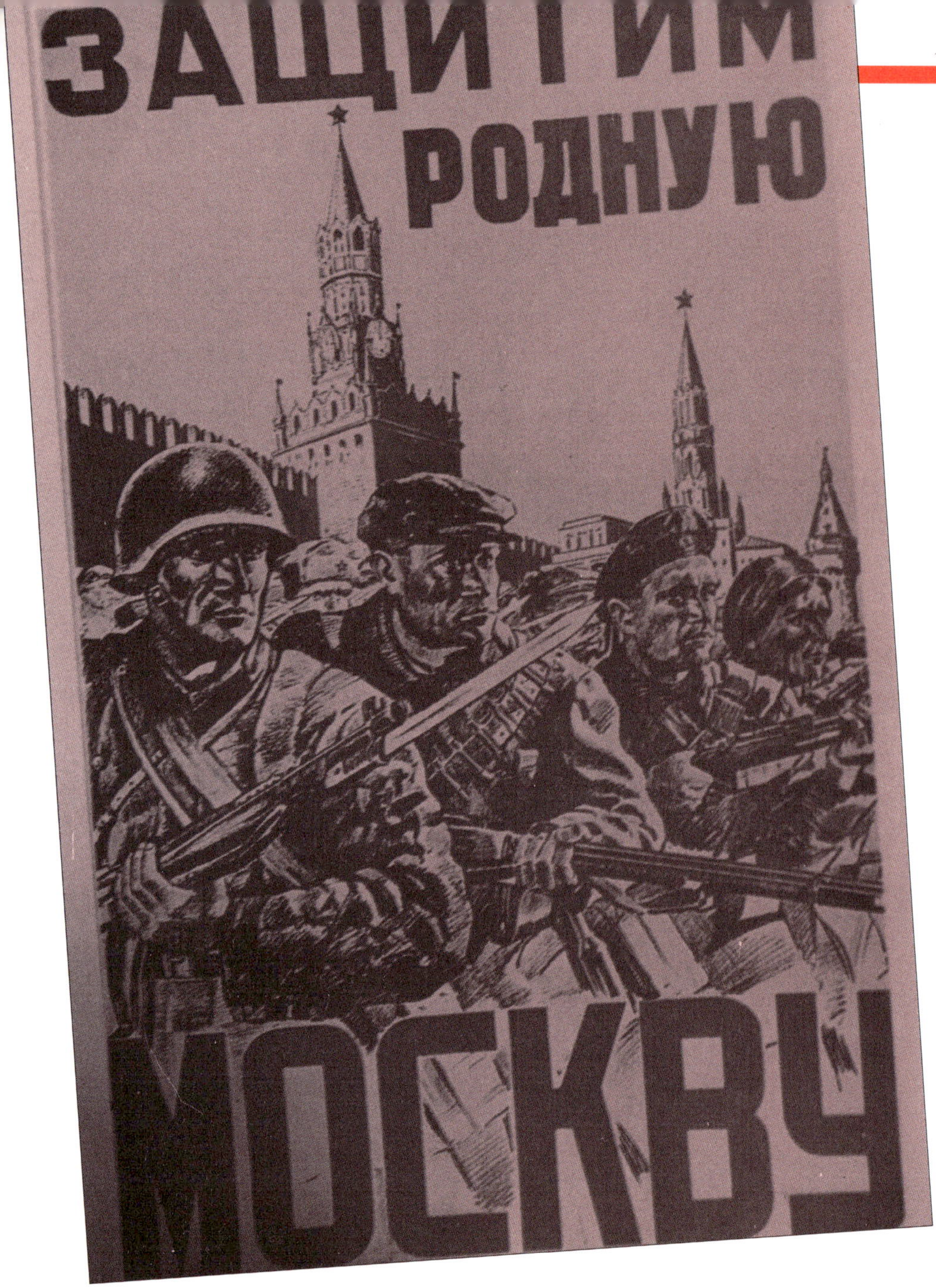

Above: **Farm workers and factory hands were called on to defend their country alongside Russia's soldiers, as the German onslaught swept in from the west.**

trundling into Russia in a three-pronged attack. The 2,500,000 Germans in the invasion force were not alone. Lining up with them were divisions of Romanians, Hungarians, Italians and Finns. There was even a Spanish unit involved. Before the attack was launched there was no formal declaration of war.

At first it was the by-now familiar story of Blitzkrieg. Panzer divisions ploughed through the Russian countryside heading for Kiev, Leningrad and Moscow. Occasionally the dirt-track roads were difficult to pass and local communications poor. Yet nothing stopped the motorised units for long. In their wake the infantry marched at a pelt, straining to keep up with the successful advance and mopping up resistance along the way.

They picked up thousands of prisoners, many caught by the rear sweep of the advance unit which snared them in a bag. Stalin, who believed that being on the offensive was the only answer to Germany's aggression, engineered some of the major military disasters of the entire conflict when he refused to allow his men to retreat.

Hundreds of planes in the sizeable Red Air Force were immediately knocked out. All was going according to plan for Germany. It seemed like the army would be at the gates of Moscow in six weeks as forecast by the enthusiastic Hitler.

Yet within a month the Soviets began fighting back. Their resolve began stiffening, their exploits became harder to contain. In fact, the Russian soldier proved a formidable enemy in combat because he was prepared to

◆ EYE WITNESS ◆

Major Chester 'Chet' Hansen, aide to US Lieutenant-General Bradley, witnessed some of the fall-outs between the American commanders and Montgomery.

‘I often quote Eisenhower who used to say Monty was a good man to serve under, a difficult man to serve with and an impossible man to serve over. We were serving with him and he certainly was a very difficult man.

His head was turned at El Alamein. He became rather vain and found it impossible to imagine he could be wrong. He tended to be chauvinistic. We felt he treated us as colonials.

He was a good commander in set metal situations. In a mobile situation we thought he was rather slow to move and tidy up the battlefield. Perhaps if we had been in the war as long as the British and taken the casualties they had we would have been a lot more cautious too.

Monty was a good division commander, it was just his personality at fault. He believed he should have been overall commander of all the ground forces in Europe. He looked on Eisenhower as incompetent. He felt Eisenhower didn't have a feel for the battle.

He offended and irritated everyone, particularly Eisenhower – to such an extent that Eisenhower once threatened to quit. It is understandable as these were very strong men. They all had their views – and they differed.’

fight to the death. His willingness to make the ultimate sacrifice became particularly apparent as the war progressed. The Germans treated their Soviet prisoners with callous contempt. They were given fewer rations than other Allied prisoners of war and there was a catalogue of cruelty and atrocities. During the war, a staggering 3,300,000 Soviet prisoners of war died in German custody.

DEATH SQUADS

When the Russians got to hear of the treatment being meted out to their comrades they fought harder than ever. There was also increased incentive to fight to the last, as they knew that imprisonment would be worse than death. Equally, anything construed as cowardice by the soldiers and failure by their commanding officers led to execution by death squads of their fellow countrymen.

At the end of July Hitler made a controversial decision which perhaps cost him the war in Russia. Concerned at the rapid pace of the Panzers compared with the slow-moving infantry, he ordered a change in tack which had the advance units of his campaign veering off in another direction. The effect of this was to give the big cities valuable time to defend themselves.

His leaders in the field were mystified and outraged. In particular, General Heinz Guderian, who stood only 220 miles from Moscow, sought to disentangle himself from the order.

When the surge forward began again, the first winter chill began to creep into the air

Above: **In 1941, before winter set in, Third Reich forces were entrenched in battles on the outskirts of Moscow, shaking the foundations of the Kremlin itself.**

But despite some initial hesitation, Hitler was convinced he was right. It caused a flurry of resignations from his senior commanders, who knew instinctively that the time was right to press forward for Moscow. With the shelter the city offered to an army, the icy arctic winter might just be tolerable. Without it, the German hierarchy – who could only guess at the ravages such a winter would hold – gave an involuntary shiver.

When the surge forward began again, the first winter chill began to creep into the air.

By September, Riga, Minsk, Smolensk and Kiev had fallen. A record 665,000 soldiers were taken prisoner when Kiev collapsed, the

Left: **German soldiers quickly began to realise the perils of fighting in a Russian winter when thick snow disabled much of their machinery.**

most ever taken during a single wartime operation. (Stalin ignored the advice of one of his most seasoned officers to evacuate the area before it was too late.) Leningrad, like Sevastopol in the Crimea, was under siege. Western Russia was pock-marked with destruction. Stalin had ordered a 'scorched earth' policy among his men which meant retreating armies torched everything in their wake to both hinder the enemy and deprive them of possible supplies.

The residents of Moscow and Leningrad had not wasted their unexpected breathing space that summer. An army of women, old men and children spent their every waking hour digging in. Between them they provided the key spots with miles of earthworks, anti-tank ditches, barbed-wire walls and pill-boxes.

An army of women, old men and children spent their every waking hour digging in

TRENCHFOOT

During their labours, their spirits must have lifted with the first deluge of autumn. The Germans, now wearying, depleted in numbers and burdened by casualties, looked up to the same endless grey skies with despair. The spring and autumn rains brought about cases of 'trenchfoot' – the vile affliction the Americans call 'immersion-foot'. The condition occurred when wet feet were not dried out for days or weeks on end. Numbed and uncomfortable, the infected feet frequently turned purple and, in severe cases, the nerve endings died and gangrene set in. Trenchfoot was to plague the Italian, American and British armies later in the war as they battled in Europe.

The Russian roads, pitted and broken at the best of times, now turned into mires of mud. The German Panzers were literally bogged down and progressed at a painfully slow pace. Mechanical failures began to haunt each division as its desperate soldiers fought to keep the wheels turning.

HITLER'S LONELY LOVER

Eva Braun spent 12 years as mistress to the hypnotic German Führer and no more than a few hours as his wife.

Braun probably began her bizarre relationship with Hitler as early as 1931. Yet he refused to accord her the public recognition she desired despite his apparent regard for her.

Much of their relationship was spent apart, with the sporty, attractive Braun, born in 1910, waiting for Hitler to finish his state commitments before squeezing in some time with her. Hitler's chauffeur described her afterwards as 'the unhappiest woman in Germany. She spent most of her life waiting for Hitler.'

Even after her sister married General Fegelein, a member of Himmler's staff, she was unable to persuade Hitler to formalise their relationship. She attempted suicide twice, in 1932 and 1935, on account of Hitler's involvement with other women.

On 15 April 1945 Eva Braun arrived in Berlin to join Hitler for what were clearly his final days. In the early hours of 29 April they were wed. The following afternoon they were dead, Hitler having shot himself and Braun having taken poison. Her body, clad in a dark dress, was placed in a shell hole at the rear of the Berlin bunker and set ablaze alongside that of her husband.

The frosts of October came as a relief to the Germans. At least the ground was hard enough to support the tank tracks, and the stride towards Moscow quickened.

Haunted by the fate of the French emperor Napoleon back in 1812, who also made mighty advances into Russia only to be crippled by the winter freeze, Hitler declared that Moscow was to be taken.

OPERATION TYPHOON

The final thrust of 'Operation Typhoon' brought German troops tantalisingly close to their goal. Some reports insist the leading units penetrated a suburb of the capital and saw sunlight glinting on the roof of the Kremlin itself. Even now they were able to take 660,000 more Russian prisoners. But their progress was slowed and finally halted.

By now 200,000 members of the Germany army had been killed. The surviving German soldiers were no longer fresh and energetic. Five months of fighting had taken its toll even among those who were not injured. The resistance they found among the defenders of Moscow was fierce, the military machinery they relied on for spearheading their attack was failing. And now the relentless winter had set in, bringing with it snow storms and temperatures of minus 20 degrees Celsius.

German soldiers were inadequately clothed for the biting cold. The greatcoats they wore were scarcely thick enough to protect them from the bitter winds. In a feeble attempt to insulate themselves, they tore up paper and stuffed it inside their clothes. For snow camouflage they used bed sheets which again offered precious little warmth. Now frostbite was the worst enemy, claiming many more victims among the demoralised Germans than the fighting itself.

Vehicle oil froze unless it was kept warmed, so the Germans were unable to move at all. The fine German horses used to pull artillery and supplies perished by the thousand. Hitler had ordered 'no retreat', perhaps realising that any movement forward or backwards posed a danger to his troops. It would be three years before the supplies of winter clothing to German troops from the Reich were adequate.

The Soviet army, meanwhile, was well used to the weather. Sheepskins and furs were standard issue. Greatest among their assets were heavy-duty felt boots soon supplied in bulk by America where they were made to Russian specification. Russians knew how to care for their animals in the coldest weather; indeed, their ponies were bred hardy and tough. A squad of crack Siberian troops was being called in, experts at winter warfare and at home on a pair of skis. The fate of Moscow hung in the balance.

Now frostbite was the worst enemy, claiming many more victims than the fighting

Below: **It wasn't just the weather that was bitter. Fighting between Russia and Germany on the Eastern front was some of the bloodiest of the entire conflict.**

JAPAN'S LIGHTNING WAR

With the success of Pearl Harbor under their belts, the Japanese were eager to capitalise on the supreme advantage of surprise. Defending British, Australian and American forces were caught off-guard throughout South East Asia and the Pacific as Japan began a 'Blitzkrieg' of its own.

Key targets were Hong Kong, the Philippines, Malaya, Singapore, Burma, Thailand, the Dutch East Indies and the stepping stone islands of Wake and Guam. Each offered the new Japanese empire mineral or agricultural wealth that was badly needed, or was a necessary land-base to protect precious cargoes.

Hong Kong was the first of the British domains to fall. Only 400 miles from Japanese air bases in Formosa (now Taiwan), it was vulnerable from the outset. The defence of Hong Kong and other prestigious British outposts had suffered thanks to the war effort in other parts of the world. During 1939 and 1940, troops, ships and aircraft were sent to trouble-spots like North Africa and the Mediterranean at the expense of the far-flung colonies, which appeared to be in no imminent danger.

By August 1940, Churchill accepted the view held by service chiefs that Hong Kong was practically indefensible and that the garrison on the island could be better used elsewhere. Japanese intentions were far from clear at this point. However, perhaps with growing indications that Japan was possibly hostile, no one acted further on the recommendation. In fact, the following year the Hong Kong garrison was strengthened by the addition of two Canadian battalions. In the event, they only added to the huge numbers of prisoners taken during those early Japanese exploits.

An initial strike made by the Japanese on 8 December proved to be devastating. The Allied troops were driven back to Hong Kong city within a matter of days. For a week, the Japanese were held at bay across the water barrier. Under the cover of darkness on 18 December, the inevitable Japanese landings on Hong Kong island began. Following Churchill's declared policy, resistance was slight. A wedge was driven between the defending forces. On Christmas Day one arm surrendered. Their comrades gave up the fight a day later. For the loss of 3,000 dead and wounded the Japanese had captured Hong Kong, together with its force of nearly 12,000 men.

The Philippines were to have suffered their first Japanese air bombardment on 8 December. Although not an American possession, they were reliant on US support before becoming independent. In fact, morning fog grounded the aircraft based in Formosa, delaying take-off.

The Americans, meanwhile, were debating whether or not to carry out a bombing mission in Formosa. The indecision proved fatal. In the early afternoon, when the US B-17s were finally being prepared for a sortie, the overdue Japanese aircraft finally arrived. With the American planes presented on an airfield, the Japanese pilots did their destructive worst. A number of the planes intended to protect the Philippines were wrecked.

For the loss of 3,000 dead and wounded the Japanese had captured Hong Kong

Left: Victorious Japanese troops enter Rangoon after quickly annihilating opposition troops in Burma. The Burmese people gave them an indifferent welcome.

Above: Dejected British soldiers file through the streets of Singapore after the disastrous fall of the colony to the Emperor's forces.

RATIONS

Rations were boosted – and cut – for Britons on the home front throughout the war. Here is a typical weekly allowance per person.

8oz sugar, 3oz cheese
3oz cooking fat, 4oz bacon or ham
2oz jam, 2oz sweets, 2oz tea or coffee
1 egg, 3 pints milk, 1lb meat

Bread, fish and sausages, although not rationed, were scarce. Although there was no restriction on fruit and vegetables, many were impossible to get. Lemons, bananas, onions and even pepper were rarely, if ever, seen during the war years in Britain.

Inventive housewives made chocolate truffle cake from potatoes, and banana pudding from parsnips.

Right: **General-Marshal Homma makes an assisted landing on Luzon in the Philippines on 24 December 1941, ousting defending American troops.**

The Japanese 14th Army quickly captured off-islands and made landings on Luzon, the largest Philippine island, as early as 10 December. There were continuing probes until the main landings, which took place on 22 December.

Coastal defences, comprising poorly trained and fearful Filipinos soon crumbled. A core of American troops was kept in the capital, Manila, by commander General MacArthur until it became clear that the defence of the island was an impossibility. He then ordered a withdrawal into the Bataan Peninsula in the hope the 31,000 troops could mount an adequate defence.

The Americans did manage to repel a number of raids. Then both sides became severely weakened through rampant malaria. Morale sank further in the American ranks when it became clear there was little or no effort being made to evacuate them. When the Japanese offensive began again on 3 April it took only six days to force a surrender.

There remained almost 15,000 Americans on the nearby island of Corregidor. The fight for this scrap of an island was to be fierce. The Japanese carried out daily artillery bombardments across the straits from Luzon as well as waves of air attacks. When much of the American artillery had been knocked out, the Japanese mounted an invasion with 2,000 troops. More than half were lost in the battle that ensued during the night of 5 May. But despite their losses, the Japanese managed to land some tanks, enough to crush the remaining resistance.

Coastal defences, comprising poorly trained and fearful Filipinos, soon crumbled

A surrender bid by American General Wainwright was hampered by guerrilla action adopted by the Americans. By 9 June, however, all resistance was crushed.

The loss to the Americans had been considerable; likewise to the native forces. A combined total of 95,000 were taken captive by the Japanese. Yet the defenders had held out for six months with no outside assistance, a significant achievement given the domino fall of islands in the rest of the area.

On paper, it appeared the British defenders of Malaya and neighbouring Singapore were more than a match for the invaders. There were about 100,000 Allied troops taking on just 30,000 incoming Japanese. In Britain there was confidence that Singapore particularly was a fortress with stout defences. It was unthinkable that the stronghold would be overrun. As so often happens during wars, the unthinkable happened – at speed.

The defeat of the British and Allied forces at the hands of the Japanese was a shocking one for which few at home were prepared. Yet there were shortcomings in the defences of the countries invaded which allowed the enthusiastic Japanese to run rampant.

Despite the signs of militarism evident in Japan, the British government remained convinced this small country would not take on the combined might of America, Britain and Russia. After the war, Churchill admitted he among others had underestimated the threat posed by Japan, particularly in its air power.

The Allies had no tanks with which to blast the enemy while the Japanese rolled over the inhospitable terrain with something in the order of 300. And while the Allies possessed more than twice the amount of artillery, much of it was in Singapore facing seawards to repel a southerly invasion. The Japanese flooded in from the opposite direction.

OPPRESSIVE HEAT

As for aircraft, the Allies had only a sixth of the number of aircraft that the Japanese had at their disposal. In a war which proved air might was imperative, the British were left seriously underequipped.

Moreover, Japanese troops were trained for jungle warfare and the dense vegetation and steamy atmosphere did not daunt them. The British and Australians were quickly wearied by the oppressive heat.

In command of the Japanese was General Tomoyuki Yamashita, a devoted servant of Emperor Hirohito and a military marvel. Among his troops, he was known as 'the tiger'. The Allies, meanwhile, were under General Arthur Percival, held with such low regard by his men that he was called 'the rabbit'.

On the day that the prize British capital ships Prince of Wales and Repulse were sent to the bottom of the sea, Japanese forces marched into Malaya. With waves of air cover, they were quickly able to force the British down the Malay Peninsula in a rolling retreat. The highly organised invaders cut quickly through any defences they encountered. About 4,000 British troops and their equipment were stranded in central Malaya when Japanese tanks broke through their lines and seized a road

Below: **Seasoned jungle warriors, the Japanese troops found far less difficulty operating in the tropics than their beleaguered enemies did.**

WAVELL VICTORIOUS

When British and Commonwealth troops under the command of General Sir Archibald Wavell drove Italian troops into a spectacular retreat early in 1941, there was rejoicing at home at the first glimpse of meaningful victory. The *News Chronicle* wrote:

'It is still too early for any complete estimate of General Wavell's happy and glorious achievement; but from what we already know two factors stand out and demand the most generous praise: the perfect co-ordination of land, sea and air forces and the superb Staff work that preceded the attack and made the co-ordination possible.'

Somewhat prematurely, it ended:
'Rapidly the Axis is becoming a meaningless phrase: an axis requires two ends, and, if it is to function, each end must perform an equal task. Otherwise the whole thing crumbles away. One day that will happen, and General Wavell, by his care and genius, has brought that day nearer than two months ago we dared hope.'

bridge, curtailing their withdrawal. The capital, Kuala Lumpur, was abandoned by the Allies on 11 January and still the retreat continued to gather pace.

MALAYA FALLS

It took the Japanese just 54 days to overcome the resistance in Malaya. Their casualties amounted to around 4,600, compared with the loss of 25,000 Allied troops, many of whom were now prisoners of war. Thousands of Indians recruited to fight for the Empire already had doubts about the wisdom of risking their lives for the country which oppressed their own. Now many took the opportunity to join brigades organised by the Japanese and were fighting against former comrades.

Fleeing British and Australian forces made a dash for Singapore and blew up the bridge connecting the island with Malaya as they went. Japanese forces mustered threateningly on the other side.

Singapore was bombed on the day the war with Japan began. The casualties were mostly among the civilian population yet it forcefully illustrated the intentions of the Japanese. Perhaps for the first time, Churchill realised the folly of leaving the island of Singapore so woefully lacking in defences.

In January 1942, he declared: 'Not only must the defence of Singapore Island be maintained by every means but the whole island must be fought for until every single unit and every single strongpoint has been separately destroyed. Finally, the city of Singapore must be converted into a citadel and defended to the death. No surrender can be contemplated.' On 8 February the Japanese troops put his words to the test by swarming across the Johore Strait which had so far barred them from the island. Some used small boats and dinghies. Others simply swam across. The Australian defenders in the region might have been expected to use the spotlights especially installed to light up their targets and blast the invaders out of the water.

Yet the order to switch on the lights never came. The soldiers were left firing at darkened objects in the night. Not only that, the troops were soon ordered to fall back rather than to counter-attack. It was a symptom of the faulty lines of communication that dogged the short campaign by the Allies to keep Singapore. The standard of leadership among the

The soldiers were left firing at darkened objects in the night

Right: **A Japanese artillery detachment making its way through the jungle in late 1941 during the Singapore campaign. They found little standing in their way.**

◆ EYE WITNESS ◆

Bill Jenkins, from New South Wales, served in the Australian infantry from the outbreak of World War II to its close.

‘My battalion and another one from Victoria were probably the only Allied units to have fought all its enemies. We were up against the Italians in the desert, the Germans in Greece, the Vichy French in Syria and the Japanese in New Guinea.

The Japanese were the worst. They were a different culture – you didn't know what to expect next from them. No prisoners were taken on either side and they were very vicious. Yet the Japanese were good soldiers. I have got much respect for them but not for their culture which allows them to do such terrible things.’

Above: **US soldiers surrender to Japanese troops. Ahead of them is a gruelling march to a harsh prison camp.**

Allies was also continually poor, with tactical blunders being made time and again. Ill-thought-out orders to withdraw from strongly held positions around the coast gave the Japanese an open door. All of this did nothing to buck the spirits of the beleaguered Allied soldiers wondering why they were left without the benefit of air cover.

SINGAPORE SHAME

Nor did the sight of thick black smoke rising over Singapore city do much to improve their state of mind. It plumed from oil tanks set alight by the British themselves in the harbour area to keep them from falling into Japanese hands. From it came a pungent black rain which fell across a wide area. A flurry of activity by Japan's supporters in Singapore added to the chaos and confusion in the city.

Food stocks were running low and the water supply was under threat by the time street battles commenced. Percival realised that to proceed with the fight was futile. A package air-dropped to his headquarters in a cascade of red and white ribbons invited him to surrender. It bore the following sinister sentence from Yamashita: ‘If you continue resistance, it will be diffcult to bear with patience, from a humanitarian point of view.’

He chose to ignore Churchill's orders to fight to the bitter end. Percival marched to meet the triumphant Yamashita with a Union Jack and a white flag, held aloft side-by-side. The close proximity of the national flag and the symbol of surrender did nothing to endear him to the establishment at home. His signature ended the British domination of Singapore at a conference held in the Ford factory on Bukit Timah hill. Some 80,000 British, Indian and Australian troops were snared, forced to face four years of gruelling captivity under the harsh Japanese regime. With the loss of Singapore came the bitter realisation that Britain's proud boast of being able to defend its colonies no matter where they were in the world was now a sham.

Afterwards, it was described as ‘the greatest military disaster in [British] history’. For years Percival was an outcast, held personally responsible for the loss of a glittering prize. While his leadership was certainly flawed, he was only one of many Allied commanders who found themselves bowled over by the Japanese steamroller.

The extent of the Singapore debacle was only revealed fully after the war when Yamashita revealed he considered himself on the brink of losing the vital campaign: ‘My attack

Right: Japanese soldiers soon adapted in the jungle, making use of local elephants to forge a path through dense vegetation. The Allied defenders could not match the invaders proficiency in jungle warfare. *Below:* General Tomoyuki Yamashita, one of Japan's most successful military leaders, pulled off a dramatic coup when he captured Singapore.

on Singapore was a bluff. I had 30,000 men and was outnumbered more than three to one. I knew that if I had been made to fight longer for Singapore I would have been beaten. That was why the surrender had to be immediate. I was extremely frightened that the British would discover our numerical weakness and lack of supplies and force me into disastrous street fighting. But they never did. My bluff worked.'

December 1941 also saw the invasion of Burma. It was inadequately protected, with Malaya and Singapore seen as having greater requirement for military resources. Once again, Japan had by far the most effective air force. It was to be another story of inglorious retreat, this time over 1,000 miles into India.

The Burmese capital Rangoon was being bombed by Christmas. The British forces were once again forced back under the onslaught of the 35,000 invading Japanese troops, who proved themselves faster and more adept in jungle warfare. On 6 March 1942 the order came to evacuate Rangoon.

MONSOON SEASON

After both sides had reinforced, the British, assisted now by Chinese forces, defended a 150-mile line south of Mandalay. The Japanese merely sidestepped the line and enveloped the troops manning it. By now it was April and the British troops not only had to consider the advance of the enemy but also the onset of the monsoon season, due in May, which would turn the roads vital for retreat into mires. Burmese soldiers, always unhappy about the colonial control of their country, were deserting in droves to join the new national army that was fighting with the Japanese invaders.

British rearguard forces held up the Japanese advance before making the final dash for safety themselves. The tanks of the 7th Armoured Brigade made repeated counter-attacks to delay the enemy campaign.

Burmese soldiers, always unhappy about the colonial control of their country, were deserting in droves to join the new national army

A week before the monsoon season began, the majority of the British forces fell back exhausted and relieved behind the Indian frontier. They had lost much of their equipment and had suffered three times the number of casualties that the Japanese had incurred. But given their circumstances, it was a miracle that any succeeded in escaping at all.

EYE WITNESS

Hugh Trebble, a local newspaper journalist, joined the Civil Air Guard before the war when it offered the chance to learn to fly for one penny per minute. In 1940 he was recruited into the Royal Air Force, in which he was a clerk.

'I was posted overseas in June 1941 and got to Singapore by August. From there I went to RAF Butterworth, overlooking Penang Island in north west Malaya. One of our first instructions when we got to Butterworth was that between 2pm and 4pm you were either in bed or out of barracks. It was impossible to raise a British officer during that time on the peninsula.

There was a lot of personnel in Malaya and Singapore but no equipment. At Butterworth we were still flying old-fashioned Bristol Blenheims. I never saw any combat aircraft the entire time I was there. Our junior officers were principally Australian.

After the Japanese invaded down the east coast we were pulled back to Kuala Lumpur to a base called Sungeibesi. A few weeks later General Wavell flew in to assess the situation. As soon as his Hudson took off we blew it [the base] up. We retreated via a rubber plantation down to Singapore.

There, we were put in a camp at RAF Seletar. There were hundreds of us that couldn't be gainfully employed. The last flight of so-called bombers that set off from there was made up of obsolete Vickers Wildebeest, twin-engined bi-planes. They took off but they never landed. They were destroyed before they could put down.

There was a desperate atmosphere in Singapore, even more so after the battleships *Prince of Wales* and *Repulse* were sunk. When they left port it was with a total absence of air cover and destroyer cover. They should never have been sent out in the first place.

In Singapore there were fixed guns facing over the sea – when the Japanese came overland. They didn't need fifth columnists in the city to help them. Japanese soldiers easily overpowered anything we had.

Some Allied soldiers got off troop ships and were taken prisoner virtually straightaway. They never fired a shot in anger. They had nothing to do any fighting with anyway.

On 13 January 1942 I was among many who were evacuated from Kepple Harbour on the *Empire Star*, a Blue Funnel ship, heading for Java. Clearly, we were sent to Singapore for propaganda purposes – nothing else.'

The Dutch East Indies came under attack in December 1941, too. This arc of wealthy islands, at its easterly point just 300 miles from the coast of Australia, was rich in oil and thus an important target for the oil-starved Japanese. In a bid to halt the Japanese, the defending Dutch, Australian, British and American forces were put under a single command, known as ABDA, led by Britain's General Archibald Wavell.

Although the Dutch resistance was soon annihilated, the Australians proved a more formidable foe. Yet there was little they could do to protect the scores of tiny islands from Japanese occupation.

After the disastrous Battle of the Java Sea, which the Allies lost in February 1942, the Japanese could count the Dutch East Indies as their own.

EYES ON CEYLON

Other casualties in the Japanese lightning war were Guam, Wake Island and the Gilbert Islands, which fell before the end of 1941. In the spring of 1942, the Bismarck Archipelago, the Solomon Islands and north eastern New Guinea all succumbed to Japanese forces.

Britain now feared attack from the Japanese navy in the Indian Ocean, where Ceylon was a prime target. Strategically, it was crucial to the British. On 5 April 1942 the British braced themselves for attack following an air strike by more than 1,000 planes at Colombo, the capital of Ceylon. Two British cruisers were sunk and the port was badly damaged. The distances were too great for an invasion to be sustainable, however, and the Japanese knew it. They withdrew behind the lines of their expanded empire and concentrated on defence.

Britain now feared attack from the Japanese navy in the Indian Ocean, where Ceylon was a prime target

THE EASTERN FRONT

Winter weather had brought the German advance in Russia to a standstill. Yet Stalin knew that freezing temperatures and snow flurries alone would not be enough to defeat the might of the Third Reich's army.

He was neither a gifted tactician nor a seasoned campaigner, unlike his enemy Hitler. In personal command of his army, Stalin was isolated at the top. The blunders he made as the barbarous campaign against his country got underway cost millions of lives. He would soon learn by bitter experience about how to run a war.

He enjoyed a certain degree of good luck and, in time, he used it well. To his advantage, he had a seemingly inexhaustible supply of men.

After Pearl Harbor, Stalin realised Japan was too embroiled with its actions against America to now threaten Russia. So the men tied up with defending its eastern rear were at last free to man the German front. In addition, there were countless thousands of reservists, recruited from all over the Soviet Union, to replace fallen comrades.

It was this perpetual sacrifice of men above all other factors that changed the course of the war. If Stalin had found his people with less resolve and more ready to capitulate, Hitler might have won on the Eastern front. And a victory there would have ensured him triumph in the west. D-Day, the single most decisive action of the entire war, could not have gone ahead without the Russian front diverting so many German resources.

D-Day could not have gone ahead without the Russian front diverting German resources

Somehow this massive country survived its appalling casualty rate. It prompted the frustrated German chief of staff Halder to comment: 'We estimated that we should contend with 180 Russian divisions; we have already counted 360.'

Wherever possible, the Soviet Union's heavy industry was moved nut by nut and bolt by bolt to the east

Above: **The half-frozen mud is littered with the bodies of dead Russian soldiers. Total Soviet losses, military and civilian, in the war may have exceeded 20 million.**

Left: **Resignation is etched on the face of a German soldier on the Eastern front, more than two years after 'Barbarossa'.**

Above: A smouldering tank is stopped in its tracks during the campaign, its crew almost certainly dead inside.

of the country to prevent it being swallowed up in the German advance – from here productivity was now stepped up. While the Germans suffered from privation, with inadequate supplies being ferried along overstretched lines beginning in occupied Poland and beyond, the Russian forces had their needs seen to swiftly and without hindrance along railway tracks still running into Moscow despite the conflict.

Key among the Russian supplies was the new T-34 tank, heavily armoured, fast and tough. It was equal if not superior to the tanks being driven by the Germans. By 1943 Russian industry was able to produce twice as many tanks as its German counterpart.

MARSHAL ZHUKOV

Russia also received fresh stocks from the Allies. Perhaps the most significant of these was a mammoth consignment of trucks from America. It enabled Stalin to move men around his huge country at increased speed. He had a fine commander in the field in Georgi Zhukov, whose military genius shone out from the floundering incompetents left at the top of what remained of the Red Army.

When they arrived they would face a quick court martial before being shot

Zhukov joined the Tsar's army as a conscript at the outbreak of World War I, aged 18, winning two medals before the Bolshevik revolution. By 1919 he was in the Red Army and a Communist Party member. A personal rapport with Stalin saved him during the military purge of 1937. He remained one of the few generals able to speak his mind to the Soviet dictator, although on at least one occasion he was demoted as a result of doing so.

RETREAT AND DIG

Not all the other Russian generals were so lucky. After war broke out, Stalin habitually telephoned commanders who had been compelled to pull back their armies and summoned them to Moscow. When they arrived they would face a quick court martial before being shot for dereliction of duty. Stalin was the only leader of World War II who continued with the outdated notion of shooting generals for failure in the field.

That was not the only old-fashioned element of warfare evident in Russia. Russian generals were forced on the offensive by Stalin no matter what the odds, as it was the

Below: Marshal Zhukov (left) pores over a battle plan as high-ranking Russians grapple with modern warfare techniques.

RICKY

In the treacherous task of clearing minefields, the British invasion force used specially trained dogs. When the dog sat down it was clear to his handler that a mine had been sniffed out.

Welsh sheepdog Ricky was clearing a canal bank in Holland when a mine blew up just three feet away from him. Ricky was wounded in the face while the blast killed the section commander. Regardless of his injuries, Ricky returned to his duties and found several more mines before retiring for treatment.

His courage won him the Dickin Medal, created by the People's Dispensary for Sick Animals, to recognise the courage of animals in the front line. Inscribed on it are the words 'For gallantry, we also serve'. Ribbons attached to the disc are green, brown and blue to represent sea, land and sky.

only way he knew of achieving victory. Devoid of any inspiration until the arrival of Zhukov and his protégés, they would send waves of men 'over the top' to hurl themselves at the Germans, much as soldiers did during the trench warfare of 1914-18. The unfortunate troops were cut down in waves.

It took Stalin at least a year to realise that his strategies were fatally flawed. When he began lending an ear to the new breed of generals, he finally realised that technique was everything in modern warfare. It was then that Russia began to turn the tables on its foe.

MOSCOW REPRIEVED

After an inconclusive Russian counter-offensive out of Moscow in December 1941, both sides suspended operations until May 1942 to give themselves valuable time to recoup men and hardware. Moscow was at least saved from occupation but its people still suffered the deprivations of war.

While Stalin was convinced Moscow remained the Third Reich's prime target, Hitler had other ideas. The need for more resources for his spiralling war effort became more pressing. He eyed the Soviet oilfields in the Caucasus greedily, knowing that success in capturing such prized assets would not only buoy Germany but would deprive Stalin of precious fuel resources as well.

Code-named 'Operation Blue', Hitler's drive east began at the beginning of May. In characteristic style, the thrust was dynamic and 170,000 Russians were taken prisoner in the first week. Two Russian counter-attacks ended in disarray. The first German objective, to take the tank-making town of Kharkov, was achieved by the end of June.

But frustration followed victory as the Germans lost the initiative when they became involved in a battle for the city of Voronezh. Russian fight-

Below: **Prepared for invasion. Moscow was lined with anti-tank devices to halt Hitler's progress in the capital.**

ers, released from the order to stay their ground by Stalin, could finally strike and then melt away, causing the maximum damage and nuisance to the Germans.

It delayed the German stab towards Stalingrad, the gateway to the Caucasus, which Hitler had earmarked as his own.

In October the German 6th Army finally reached Stalingrad and launched a bloody offensive with the aid of endless strikes by the Luftwaffe. Russian defenders of the city adopted the tactics of guerrilla warfare, going underground to snipe at the oncoming Germans.

OPERATION URANUS

Even as the winter set in, German commander Paulus braced himself and his men for a final effort, during November 1942. Although the killing went on, he achieved little.

But now the Russians were to bring into play some of the devastating tactics they had learned the hard way, at the hands of the invading Germans. Paulus found his flanks surrounded by a mighty Russian force ready to put a noose around the weakened 6th Army. This was Stalin's 'Operation Uranus', devised between himself, Zhukov and Chief of General Staff Vasilevsky.

When he heard about the disaster, Hitler was furious. He pledged supplies would be dropped by the Luftwaffe to the beleaguered Paulus and organised a relief column. But he refused to give Paulus the lifeline he needed for himself and his men – the order to break out of the encirclement or retreat.

EYE WITNESS

Dennis Golding, of Gosport, near Portsmouth, England, was a British rifleman with the King's Royal Rifle Corps. As a light infantryman he was engaged in hand-to-hand combat with German troops throughout the 1944 advance across western Europe.

"There are still so many myths about the war. If one of our men was wounded in an attack we didn't all stop and gather around him like you see in the movies. We didn't have time to think about it. We just carried on and completed our assignment.

Of course, you would help if you could. But it took four men to deal with one man wounded and you could end up going nowhere.

Then again I saw soldiers who didn't even realise they had been hit. It was only when one of their mates pointed out blood seeping through their uniform that they felt the pain.

Cracking up under fire is another aspect surrounded in mythology. Everybody thinks of these guys running away. I saw one lance corporal who just got up and wandered, babbling, straight into enemy fire. He was what we called bomb happy, or shell-shocked. We never found his body.

I came across the same symptoms affecting Germans who surrendered to us after we took the Falaise Gap. Almost an entire German division was wiped out there and there were thousands of bodies and animal carcasses just heaped up in the streets. That was a sight no man should ever have to see.

The German troops had been shelled and bombed for days without end. By the time the Canadians and ourselves got to them they had no fight left. You could tap them on the shoulder and they would follow you; they didn't know or care where you were taking them.

We always had to be alert. Once when we were clearing a forest a German infantryman popped out of his fox-hole a few yards away and levelled his gun at me. I heard one of my mates shout 'Look out Den' and then that man opened up on the German and killed him.

I'll never forget staring at his body and watching this very pale white cloud emerging from his chest, so faint you could hardly see it. Some soldiers later told me I'd seen the man's soul departing. I don't know about that. Maybe it was just another myth."

GERMANS BESIEGED

At Stalingrad the outlook for the Germans was bleak. Only a fraction of the food and medical supplies needed were being flown in. Injury or sickness accounted for as much as one fifth of the 100,000-strong force.

The Russian commanders were confident enough to offer Paulus an opportunity to surrender as early as 8 January 1943. Paulus knew the Führer would be maddened so he stood fast.

Left: **German pilots notched up some stunning successes on the Eastern front despite facing grim flying conditions.**

***Above:* Stalingrad proved a vital turning point for Germany in the war. Flouting Hitler's wishes, Third Reich troops surrendered to the Russians following a gruelling and costly winter battle.**

Another heavy bombardment rained down on Stalingrad a few days later, leaving the depleted fighting force even more demoralised and desperate. In a last-minute frantic gesture, Hitler promoted Paulus to the rank of field-marshal. Paulus knew well enough the politics behind the honour. No German field-marshal had ever surrendered. The message was clear, fight to the death.

In the misery of snow and ice, Paulus must have glanced around at some of the bodies of the thousands of German soldiers who died in those hellish weeks and wondered why.

Now Paulus found the courage to be the first field-marshal to wave a white flag. At the close of January his headquarters was overrun and he surrendered to the elated Russians. He went on to join a turncoat regiment of Germans who, following capture, fought for the Russians. For the victors there was the prize of 110,000 prisoners. For the defeated, it was unmitigated disaster.

Germans were on the run elsewhere in Russia as well, chased by an increasingly confident Red Army who were at their best in winter. It was far from the end of the war at the Eastern front. But it was the beginning of the end for Germany even if Hitler remained blind to the fact for months to come.

Now Paulus found the courage to be the first field-marshal to wave a white flag

The subsequent drive by the Russian army between January and March was fruitless. Crack German commander Field-Marshal Erich von Manstein staged a determined recovery. This small consolation did little for Hitler's morale. He was broken by the Stalingrad debacle, losing his self-confidence and intuition.

Fighting continued in explosive spats until the scene was set for a major confrontation at Kursk. Hitler allowed the planned offensive, 'Operation Citadel', to be delayed time and again while his commanders struggled to get sufficient numbers of tanks in position.

It was 5 July before the battle commenced. By 12 July there were some 2,700 German tanks and 1,800 German aircraft ranged against almost 4,000 Soviet tanks. It was the largest head-on tank battle in history, an epic test of firepower which would leave both sides battered and worn. Tank after tank went up in flames, its crew having little chance of escaping the inferno. At the end of the day there were 300 German tanks smouldering. Still more Russian tanks were burnt out but the German advance had been halted. It spelled defeat once more for the Reich. And the dramatic loss of so many tanks would take Germany many more weeks to recover than it would Russia, leaving their armoured divisions sorely lacking in firepower and mobility.

Now it was for Hitler to contemplate withdrawal. It was alien to his nature to pull out of territory fought over and won two years before. But the Red Army was flexing its muscles and was already chasing the German army out of the Crimea and the Baltic lands. The plan favoured by commanders like Manstein, to pull back to a single defensive line, soon became the only option. If only there had been enough materials and men to build the defences envisaged by Hitler, perhaps the gains he made would have been preserved at least for a while. But the Germans were unable to dig in along the 2,000-mile front and provide an effective defence. Their greatest protection to date, the ineffectiveness of the Red Army, was no longer relevant. Hitler's dream to take Russia had turned into the same nightmare that afflicted Napoleon 150 years before.

By January 1944 the Red Army was at last able to lift the siege of Leningrad. The city had been encircled since November 1941, suffering months of artillery bombardment. When liberation came after 900 days, only one third of the original population of three million were left alive.

Just as the winter of 1941-42 caused devastation among the invaders, so it brought misery and despondency to the hemmed-in people of Leningrad.

Rationing was down to just nine ounces of bread per day for working people and half that amount for those too young or too old to be employed. Cats, dogs, even rats, were eaten in a bid to stave off starvation. In front of the desperate people lay the no-man's land of defences against the Germans. Behind them lay frozen Lake Ladoga, over which there was a narrow trail into free Russia.

When liberation came after 900 days, only one third of the original population of three million were left alive

Minimal supplies found their way across the trail at first and even the smallest relief attempts were harried by German aircraft. By the spring, the residents had learned a harsh lesson. Every available inch of land was cultivated and there were fresh

DIEPPE

Twenty-one years after the disastrous raid at Dieppe which cost the lives of hundreds of Canadian servicemen, an investigation was launched to probe whether an advertisement for soap flakes gave the enemy vital advance information.

The commando raid at Dieppe in August 1942 involved 5,000 Canadians, 1,000 British, 50 American Rangers and some Free French fighters. Only half returned. The rest were killed or captured after being pinned down on the beach by the Germans. A week before it took place English newspapers carried an advertisement for Sylvan soap flakes under the title 'Beach Coat from Dieppe'. The copy afterwards read: 'How could you have known when you bought it that sunny day before the war that such a flippant little coat would be so useful about the house in war-time?'

There was speculation that in the advertisement was hidden the message 'Beach Combined Operations at Dieppe'. The woman pictured carried secateurs. Were they in fact wire cutters? Scotland Yard and MI5 swooped on the advertising agency Graham and Gillies and on the manufacturers of the soap flakes. They were persuaded it was a horrible coincidence. But no one knows whether the Germans had read the advertisement and seen secret codes where none in fact existed.

Below: **The tank battle at Kursk was an epic trial of strength. In the end it was the Russians who triumphed.**

Above: **The sight of Russian tanks lying uselessly by the roadside provide a grim spectacle for passing troops.**
Right: **Many German soldiers died as they vainly struggled to repair vehicles frozen in the snow.**

vegetables available throughout the rest of their imprisonment. Electricity was also rationed, the sewers were brim full and even clean water was in short supply.

When the saviour army lifted the blockade, they were greeted with a weary relief by the Leningraders.

Between March and April the Red Army reclaimed 165 miles of territory. Their greatest push was yet to come, however, in the form of 'Operation Bagration', which began in June, just as Hitler came under acute pressure from the D-Day landings in Normandy. Before it began, the partisans working for the Russians behind German lines set to work by setting off a series of disabling explosions.

The operation was characterised by now-familiar tactics employed by the Red Army. A burst of artillery fire to 'soften up' the enemy followed by the rapid advance of the infantry. Thousands of German soldiers were taken prisoner as Minsk fell once again to the Russians. Their humiliation was to walk down the silent streets of Moscow on their way to prison camps, watched through the narrowed, loathing eyes of the city residents. Now the German forces in the east were stretched to breaking point. Stubbornly, Hitler refused to let his troops pull back even when they had been overrun. The Führer's behaviour only offered more to the Russians by way of enemy casualties and prisoners.

By August, the Russian troops were on the Polish border. They had been forced to contend with more than three times the number of troops facing the Allies in Normandy and had proved themselves equal to the task. For the first time, the war was to be carried into Reich territory.

A FORGOTTEN ARMY

Just like the British fighters in Burma and the American soldiers assisting the Chinese, the troops who fought to regain Italy believed themselves to be 'a forgotten army'.

Theirs was a protracted campaign remembered mostly for its mud, miscalculation and unexpectedly high casualty rate. Churchill had described the Italian peninsula as 'the soft underbelly' of the Third Reich. Fierce German resistance proved his judgement to be wildly awry.

After nearly a year of strenuous fighting, the Allies took Rome on 4 June 1944. The trumpeted D-Day operations which began the following night swallowed the limelight. Forces who felt they had lost the recognition they deserved joked wryly thereafter about themselves being 'D-Day dodgers in sunny Italy'.

The opportunity to open a second front in Europe occurred when the fighting in North Africa was brought to a victorious close in 1943. For months, the Americans had been pushing for a campaign on the continent. Their chosen siting was northern France. But Churchill and his commanders felt it was premature, preferring instead to squeeze the Germans from the south.

By July 1943, the invasion of Sicily, code-named 'Operation Husky', was prepared. Montgomery was to lead his weary but able 8th Army in one assault while General Patton, heading the US 7th Army, came via a different route. The aim was to trap the defending German forces in a pincer movement.

During the course of the invasion, Italy swapped sides in the war, having overthrown the dictator Mussolini. Despite the chaos that this caused among the Germans, a staggering 40,000 were able to slip through the British and American trap and escape to the mainland.

Little did they know that the resolve of the Germans was harder than ever

Nevertheless, Sicily was in Allied possession by 17 August. An armistice was signed on 3 September as the 8th Army crossed the Straits of Messina to land in Calabria, in 'Operation Baytown'. The effect of the revelation of the Italian volte face on the troops poised to continue with the invasion of the mainland was disastrous. There were cheers and celebrations before the operation had even begun. The men believed southern Italy was theirs for the taking. Little did they know the resolve of the German defenders to stop them was harder than ever, and they were mentally ill-prepared for the brutal fighting which awaited them.

Far left: **The sky is decorated by a fireball, following a German dive-bomber attack on an American cargo ship during the invasion of Sicily.**

Left, inset: **Allied DUKW amphibious vehicles, nicknamed 'ducks', are loaded aboard a landing ship at Salerno harbour in preparation for the next phase of the invasion of Italy.**

Above: **Weary from a foot-slog in Sicily, US soldiers prop themselves up at the foot of an Italian memorial to the soldiers of World War I.**

SALERNO LANDINGS

On 9 September the next phase of the invasion began. A total of 165,000 British and American servicemen spilled out of 500 ships in a large-scale amphibious landing. The landings at Salerno, code-named 'Operation Avalanche', were scheduled by US commander General Mark Clark to last three days. He had supreme confidence in the ability of the troops to secure a quick victory. Within just 72 hours he expected Naples to have fallen, giving the Allies a crucial harbour facility. In fact, it took 21 days of gruelling battle. An attack staged at Taranto designed to divert the Germans failed. Crack German troops held the British and Americans at Salerno until reinforcements had been brought forward.

The fastidious and highly critical Montgomery, who expressed doubts about the planning of the campaign from the outset, encountered tough resistance as he and his men tried to fight their way up the toe of Italy to rendezvous with the rest of the invasion force. He was horrified to find the German positions had been reinforced. Clark's and Montgomery's troops finally made the planned link up on 16 September. In those weeks 25,000 soldiers and civilians died.

Although a first vital and substantial foothold in Italy had been carved out, the fighting didn't get any easier. The terrain of rocky peaks and steep escarpments favoured defensive positions, all of which were held by the Germans. Time and again, the Allied soldiers found themselves fatally exposed.

By 15 November the campaign was brought to a halt, hampered as it was by winter weather. Relations between the British and American commanders were equally chilly.

The next tactic to bring about a breakthrough took the form of the Allied landings at Anzio in January 1944. In 'Operation Shingle', the beachheads were quickly secured, yet the Allies had difficulty spearheading an advance. Indeed, they only narrowly missed being driven back into the sea by a determined German counter-offensive. Soon Anzio was under seige. Conflicts there were bitter. The Allies were desperately seeking routes to push forward.

Above: **Allied artillery in action against targets in Italy. The gunners, from 97 Heavy AA Regiment, Royal Artillery, feel the heat.**

By now the Allied reinforcements consisted of British, American, French, Canadian, New Zealand, South African, Greek and Brazilian troops. Even the Japanese were playing their part. The Nisei-Americans, Japanese settlers in America who had been reviled at home after Pearl Harbor, made several vital strikes on behalf of the Allies.

MONTE CASSINO

The road to Rome was marked by the architectural treasure of Monte Cassino, a sacred Christian site founded in 529 by Saint Benedict. It was filled with cultural riches gathered through the centuries, kept lovingly in archives by the monks who lived and worked at the abbey.

Perched high on a mountainous ridge, Monte Cassino looked down into the town of Cassino and away across the plains. Monastery and town were connected by a funicular railway which climbed the sheer rocky face of the peak with ease.

Cassino was in the hands of the Germans in January 1944, a major strength in its defences known as 'the Gustav line'. It became the target of Allied plane attacks but even a heavy pounding failed to eradicate the defenders. Soon, it became clear the Germans were using the abbey as a defensive stronghold, unassailable at the mountain top.

The Americans then took one of the most controversial decisions of the conflict – to bomb the delightful monastery

The Americans then took one of the most controversial decisions of the conflict – to bomb the delightful monastery which was consequently smashed to smithereens.

Little was achieved. Still Allied forces were left clinging to the mountainside, scrambling forward a few yards whenever they could. It

Right: **The German forces in Italy finally surrendered to the Allies on 2 May 1945.**

WESTERN ITALY EDITION

UNION JACK EDITION

No. 478 Two Lire

Thursday, May 3, 1945

A Million Of The Enemy Lay Down Arms

FULL SURRENDER OF NAZIS IN ITALY

ALTHOUGH fighting continues in other parts of Europe, the entire enemy forces in Italy have surrendered unconditionally to the Allies under Field-Marshal Alexander. This triumphant end to the campaign was announced last evening.

Hostilities ceased at 14.00 Italian time yesterday, when nearly a million of the enemy laid down their arms in the surrender area, which includes part of Austria.

The Italian campaign, which began with Montgomery's landing at the base of the peninsula in September 1943, has thus resulted in the first mass surrender of a complete German front.

The grand climax came after the great break-through to the Po Valley by the Fifth and Eighth Armies, aided in their sweeping advance by Italian Partisans. In three weeks the German defending forces were torn to pieces. The last act is described in this special communique from AFHQ:

Enemy land, sea and air forces commanded by Col.-Gen. Heinrich von Vietinghoff-Scheel, German C-in-C S W and C-in-C Army Group "C," have surrendered unconditionally to Field-Marshal Sir Harold Alexander, Supreme Allied Commander, Mediterranean Theatre of operations.

The terms of surrender provided for the cessation of hostilities at 12 noon GMT Wednesday, May 2, 1945.

Special Orders Of The Day

Special Orders of the Day were issued by the Allied commanders in Italy to mark the surrender.

From Field-Marshal Sir Harold ALEXANDER, Supreme Allied Commander, Mediterranean Theatre:

From Gen. Joseph T. McNARNEY, Deputy Supreme Allied Commander, Mediterranean Theatre:

From Gen. Mark W. CLARK, Commanding General, 15 Army Group:

FALL OF BERLIN

Great news also came from Germany itself last night. Marshal Stalin announced the capture of Berlin and vast numbers of prisoners in a complete rout of the garrison. (See Page 4.)

wasn't until May that the Allies by-passed the hazard, leaving the ruins of the abbey to fall to the Polish army in the rear. With heavy casualties, the Polish, assisted by a British contingent, took 1,500 prisoners – men of the German 4th Parachute Regiment.

To capture Monte Cassino, the Allies used 27 divisions with 1,900 tanks, together with 4,000 aircraft. Casualties on both sides were appalling, with some 105,000 Allied soldiers killed or wounded alongside 80,000 Germans.

FALL OF ROME

Although Rome fell soon afterwards and the incoming troops received a tumultuous welcome from its citizens, it was not the end of fighting in Italy. Still Germany threw men and ammunition at the advancing Allies. Pockets of resistance around Rimini and Bologna held the advance until the winter months, when by necessity it all but ground to a halt. Allied troops were forced to dig in during the inclement weather, experiencing the same dreadful conditions that faced their forebears in the trenches of World War I.

As late as 9 April 1945, the Allies were compelled to begin another offensive. It wasn't until 2 May that a surrender was negotiated with the weary and disillusioned Germans.

Casualties were appalling, with some 105,000 Allied soldiers killed or wounded

◆ EYE WITNESS ◆

Lieutenant-Colonel Alex Borrie was in a New Zealand brigade involved in the battle for Italy and later wrote *Escapades around Cassino*. In his diary dated 18 March 1944, he wrote:

‘Our C Company moved past Castle Hill to attack Cassino. Their main objectives were ‘Hotel des Roses’ and ‘Hotel Continental’. They were to retreat to a cave above part of the Monastery Road at 6pm. I was sent up the hill with a team of soldiers carrying food and medical supplies. The 4th Indian Division was beyond our Company on Hangman's Hill. Passing from Castle Hill to the road, the Germans put up many flares. We felt most conspicuous but the experienced soldiers said: "Stand still!" No shots were fired. At 9.10pm we reached the cave spot on time. I called out "Any Kiwis here?"

"Ssh, quiet, we just arrived ten minutes ago. There are Germans everywhere." On the way down, supplies had been dropped by parachute. Someone once said to me: "Parachutes make wonderful underpants." I tore off plenty but back at the R.A.P. it was red thick cotton – useless.’

Right: **The fierce battle at Monte Cassino left the monastery a shattered wreck.**

OVERLORD!

It was the day that Europe had been waiting for, when Allied soldiers would tread again on French soil. In the event, many had to step over the bodies of fallen comrades lying lifeless in the Normandy surf before their feet touched Nazi-occupied France.

The Americans had been pressing for an assault on occupied Europe virtually since their entry into the war. Cautious British commanders, stung by heavy losses during the trial foray onto the French coastline at Dieppe two years previously, at last thought the time was right to begin the liberation of the continent. A defeat could have been a death-blow to Britain's war effort, leaving her without an army. The commanders were finally convinced that victory was likely to be theirs.

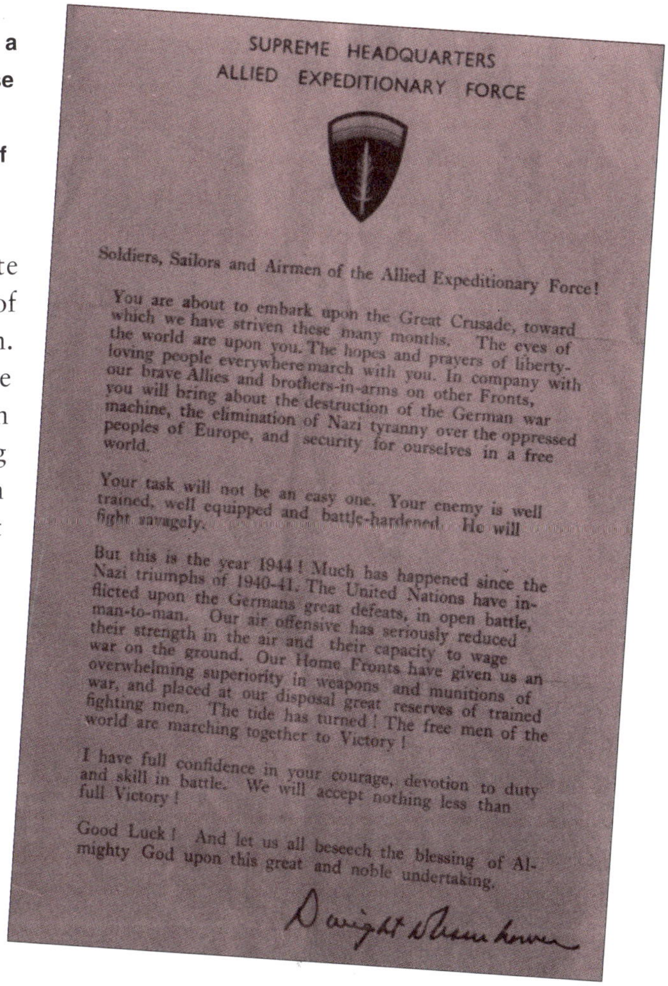

SUPREME HEADQUARTERS
ALLIED EXPEDITIONARY FORCE

Soldiers, Sailors and Airmen of the Allied Expeditionary Force!

You are about to embark upon the Great Crusade, toward which we have striven these many months. The eyes of the world are upon you. The hopes and prayers of liberty-loving people everywhere march with you. In company with our brave Allies and brothers-in-arms on other Fronts, you will bring about the destruction of the German war machine, the elimination of Nazi tyranny over the oppressed peoples of Europe, and security for ourselves in a free world.

Your task will not be an easy one. Your enemy is well trained, well equipped and battle-hardened. He will fight savagely.

But this is the year 1944! Much has happened since the Nazi triumphs of 1940-41. The United Nations have inflicted upon the Germans great defeats, in open battle, man-to-man. Our air offensive has seriously reduced their strength in the air and their capacity to wage war on the ground. Our Home Fronts have given us an overwhelming superiority in weapons and munitions of war, and placed at our disposal great reserves of trained fighting men. The tide has turned! The free men of the world are marching together to Victory!

I have full confidence in your courage, devotion to duty and skill in battle. We will accept nothing less than full Victory!

Good Luck! And let us all beseech the blessing of Almighty God upon this great and noble undertaking.

Dwight Eisenhower

Right: **Dwight Eisenhower sent a 'good luck' message to all those who took part in 'Operation Overlord', the Allied invasion of occupied France.**

The Germans, too, had been waiting with trepidation for the day that their enemies would try to get a foothold once more in Europe and had fortified the French coastline accordingly. Construction on the lines of tunnels, guns and bunkers to protect Hitler's Europe stretching 3,000 miles from Holland to the south of France began in September 1941 and got underway in earnest when Rommel took charge of the huge task in 1943.

German intelligence was good yet they still had no idea when and how the invasion would come. Norway, the Balkans and Calais were all strong possiblities. The imminence of the invasion, however, was beyond doubt in anyone's mind.

Hitler hoped it would be Disaster-Day for the Allies, with the German defenders casting the invaders back into the sea. He guessed rightly that the outcome of the attack would decide the war. Fulfilling everybody's expectations, the invasion came in early June. 'Operation Overlord' was the culmination of more than a year's work. It was an elaborate plan involving thousands of soldiers, sailors and airmen. The troops who would be scrambling up the foreign shores and overwhelming the German opposition could only guess at what fate held in store for them when they set sail across the Channel for France.

The shortest route from Britain would, of course, have been from Dover to Calais, where German and British troops could already spy each other on clear days. For this reason, German defences were tight on that section of the French coast in readiness for an Allied invasion.

Despite the advantage of the brief crossing, the beaches around Calais posed too great a threat to the troops. Allied commanders had to look elsewhere. Further west, they found the answer to their conundrum – the long, golden beaches of Normandy. Here the German defences were comparatively thin.

Further west, they found the answer – the long, golden beaches of Normandy

Before 'Operation Overlord' got underway, there were key factors to consider which would help the Allies win the battle – and triumph in the war. First was the training of the men involved. Although amphibious landings had already been tried and tested during the war, nothing of the same magnitude had ever been attempted. British, American and Canadian soldiers were posted around Britain for rehearsals.

Coastal resorts like Woolacombe, Gosport, Westward Ho!, Salcombe, Studland Bay and Slapton Sands played host to hundreds of soldiers sent to practise beach landings in an environment similar to that which they would encounter in France.

Slapton became a scene of disaster when live ammunition killed some of the soldiers taking part. Then, on 28 April 1944, mass devastation was wreaked when German E-boats slunk into a convoy in training off the coast, sinking two landing craft and killing 749 soldiers and sailors.

Left: **When Utah beach was secured, troops and supplies flooded ashore from the scores of ships in the Channel.**

'OPERATION OVERLORD'

During the night of 5/6 June 1944, the armada carrying 21st Army Group – the 'Operation Overlord' strike force – approached the coast of Normandy. The assault was to be concentrated on five beaches: the two in the west (code-named 'Utah' and 'Omaha') were the responsibility of the Americans under Bradley; the three in the east ('Gold', 'Juno' and 'Sword') were the target of the British under Dempsey. The army group was under the overall command of Montgomery. Early in the morning of the 6th, the reconquest of continental Europe began as the first Allied forces hit the beaches and struggled to establish beachheads. German resistance was tough, but the liberation was underway.

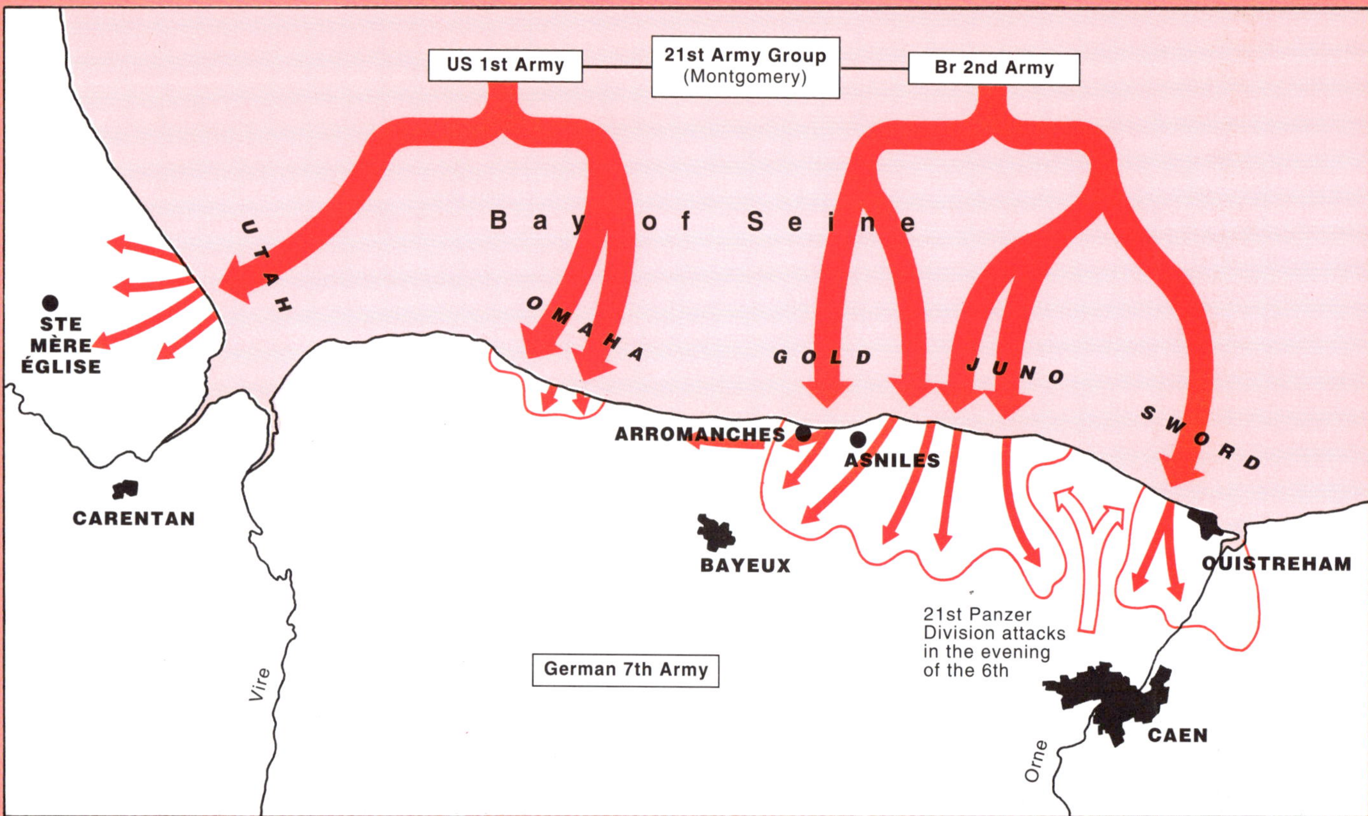

Support for the soldiers and sailors promised to be greater than anything known before. Construction firms all over the United Kingdom set to work on a top secret engineering project, each company manufacturing a different component for a giant concrete jigsaw. Few of the workers involved could guess that they were building massive harbours called 'Mulberries', to be towed across to France for docking purposes by 150 tugs. Now the invading forces didn't have to capture a ready-built harbour, always a costly exercise in terms of human lives. Tanks, trucks, big guns and supplies would roll along the Mulberries with ease.

PLUTO

A pipeline under the ocean (code-named 'Pluto'), made from steel or sometimes steel and lead, was installed to bring essential fuel quickly from Britain to France; it was laid on the sea bed by slow-moving tugs. After the war, it was salvaged to provide plumbing for 50,000 houses.

Reconnaissance was meticulously detailed. Air force pilots flying Spitfires stripped of ammunition to make them as speedy as possible photographed as much of the coastline as they could. In addition, an appeal for holiday photographs and postcards of the region reaped thousands of pictures of the area. Further aided by maps provided by the French Resistance, cartographers began to build up a three-dimensional impression of the targeted Normandy beaches.

Midget submarines went on dangerous nightly missions to the Normandy coast. Their occupants braved the water and the German patrols to bring back soil and sand samples and up-to-date information on the position of German defences.

Last but not least the British authorities embarked on a highly detailed decoy campaign to fool the Germans, who were equally involved in reconnaissance.

Along the Kent coast, some 150 miles from the British heart of 'Overlord', there was an impressive collection of armour and shipping being prepared. Only on close inspection was it revealed that the tanks were rubber and the ships were made from plywood. Lines of tents were empty apart from army cookers puffing smoke through the chimneys to make them appear authentic. The oil depots, planes and jetties that mushroomed in the area were also shams, designed to convince the Germans that the Allied thrust would be launched against Calais.

Only on close inspection was it revealed that the tanks were rubber

'Operation Fortitude', as it was code-named, was vital to the success of the invasion. The Allied forces could still be driven back into the sea if the might of the Third Reich descended on them within the first few days of the assault. With a variety of bogus intelligence messages, the commanders behind 'Fortitude' managed to convince the Germans that the invasion in Normandy was only a diversion and that the real attack was coming at Calais. Given that information, the Germans refused to move their forces from Calais, thereby saving the Allies from an onslaught.

◆ EYE WITNESS ◆

William Ryan, of the US 16th Infantry Regiment, was in the first wave to land at Omaha beach. At 18, it was his first action. He went on to serve 30 years in the army and is a veteran of the Korean and Vietnam wars.

'We loaded up the transports at Portland, Weymouth, about 2 June. We were supposed to attack on 5 June. They cancelled it due to weather. We were on the ship all those days.

Everyone was sea-sick. At about 2am on 6 June we loaded on to small 36ft LCVPs, we were 12 miles out. They wanted to surprise the enemy. The seas were six or eight feet high. By now most of the men were so sick they didn't care whether they lived or died. They were too sick to be scared. Even coxswain was sick. I ran the boat for five miles until he started to feel better.

My company was assigned six boats. We lost two boats almost immediately – they were swamped with heavy waves. Heading for the beach the coxswain lost his bearings. When he realised we were off course he had to try again.

The guys from the next sector blew over into our beach – their boats filled the beach so we couldn't get in. We had to circle around like sitting ducks. When we finally started into the beach we lost all four boats with the fire from the German 88s.

I was blown over the side and knocked unconscious. I was told later that two of the men in the boat with me dragged me through the water and propped me up against an embankment. Otherwise I would have drowned.

At first there were five or six wounded with me. Then there were hundreds. I laid on the beach in that same position from about 8am until 10pm when they evacuated us. I had concussion in addition to shell fragments in my head, shoulder and leg. All this time I was going in and out of consciousness, looking down on Omaha beach. It was just a madhouse.

Troops were pinned down by the gun emplacements. Eventually a US Navy destroyer came in as close to the beach as possible without running aground and started firing at all the German emplacements. In a little while two or three other destroyers started shelling as well. In my opinion, that is what saved Omaha beach from defeat.

I heard afterwards the skipper on the ship was ordered to go back to a safe position. Apparently he said he wasn't leaving while US soldiers were pinned down on the beach. He could have been court martialled for what he did. But he should have got a medal.

I didn't have anything to eat all day. In the afternoon a US soldier came over the hill with a couple of bottles of French red wine which he gave to us. You are never going to beat Americans in war. They are crazy.'

Right: D-Day would not have succeeded had the Allies not had mastery of the skies. A B-26 Marauder returns home after carrying out a bombing mission unchallenged over Normandy.

A double stood in for Monty and made a public departure for Algiers – when the real Montgomery was safely ensconced in 'Overlord' headquarters, which was Southwick House, Portsmouth.

The initial landings were to be made by 156,000 men, mostly Britons, Americans and Canadians. With them was an impressive turnout from occupied Europe. The line-up included an armoured division from France, a Belgian brigade, a Dutch brigade, a Polish division, as well as multi-national seaborne forces. In the skies, the main air forces were joined by squadrons from Norway, Czechoslovakia, France, Poland, Australia and New Zealand.

More men and equipment were held in reserve for future operations in Europe. It took an armada to ferry the men for the first action across the Channel. By late May, 359 warships, 1,000 minesweepers and associated vessels, 4,000 landing craft, 805 merchantmen, 59 blockships and 300 other small craft were at the ready.

Local people became used to the sight of tanks and trucks lining the streets, as major military traffic jams built up

Overhead, more than 11,000 aircraft were assembled. Some would be towing gliders to be released over France. Each of these carried some 30 troops, tasked with tackling inland enemy positions, including vital landmarks which would halt a German advance, like Pegasus Bridge. The seas and the skies belonged to the Allies. Montgomery had promised his men that the invasion would not go ahead until that umbrella of protection was firmly in place.

Anyone living on the south coast of England could have had no doubt that an invasion was poised to go ahead. Local people became used to the sight of tanks and trucks lining the streets, as major military traffic jams built up on the main roads to Portsmouth. Now there were 1,500,000 American troops alone massed on British shores. Then, one morning, they were gone.

Beginning on 2 June, the hordes of men and machinery bound for Normandy boarded their ships. The weather had been unseasonably poor. High winds and rain had lashed southern Britain, putting the entire operation at risk. It had to be postponed once from 5 June. General Dwight Eisenhower, supreme Allied commander, considered a further postponement in the face of the driving winds and rains which could wreak havoc with a seaborne landing force. The next date in June when the tides and the light were compatible was not for almost another two weeks. Some commanders favoured waiting. Others, like Montgomery, believed the strike should go ahead. It would, after all, be impossible to keep aboard ship those men already embarked. Each soldier and marine had already been interned in a camp for at least three weeks and was primed and ready for

Above: A US ship returns to a British port loaded with 'Overlord' casualties, while in France the action continues.

action. Any postponement could only have led to a deterioration in their mental and physical fitness. Anyway, the risk of them talking once they got ashore – and giving the game away – was too great.

Eisenhower smoked and read Westerns while he pondered the dilemma. Finally he made his decision. Heartened by predictions of a break in the weather, he signalled the go-ahead for 6 June, with the words 'OK, let's go'.

IKE SPEAKS

Eisenhower, fondly known as 'Ike', gave this message to the departing men of the Allied Expeditionary Force: 'You are about to embark upon the Great Crusade, toward which we have striven these many months. The eyes of the world are upon you. The hopes and prayers of liberty-loving people everywhere march with you. In company with our brave Allies and brothers-in-arms on other Fronts, you will bring about the destruction of the German war machine, the elimination of Nazi tyranny over the oppressed peoples of Europe and security for ourselves in a free world.

'Your task will not be an easy one. Your enemy is well trained, well equipped and battle-hardened. He will fight savagely.

'But this is the year 1944! Much has happened since the Nazi triumphs of 1940-41. The United Nations have inflicted upon the Germans great defeats, in open battle, man-to-man...The tide has turned! The free men of the world are marching together to Victory.'

The only message to reach the expectant public that day was a short, sharp statement, reading: 'Under the command of General Eisenhower, Allied naval forces, supported by strong air forces, began landing Allied armies this morning on the northern coast of France.'

As the soldiers and sailors bobbed in darkness on a choppy sea, they were nervous, tense, euphoric and excitable. Some were sea-sick, some prayed, many fought an overwhelming feeling of doom. Still more found enough spirit to tell jokes. The huge size of the armada involved in 'Operation Neptune', which got them across the Channel, only served to inflate their confidence.

The troops heard the drone of aircraft overhead – a big boost to their morale. Not only were the planes going to bombard enemy positions along the coast in preparation for the landings. Some were carrying paratroopers who, in the first leg of 'Overlord', were being

EYE WITNESS

Henry 'Marty' Martin, from Chicopee, Massachusetts, USA, witnessed the tragedy of 'Operation Tiger' at Slapton Sands while training for D-Day.

'When the German E-boats attacked we just thought it was just part of the exercise. I was right in that exercise and I didn't find out for another 43 years that 749 men had drowned. These guys were wearing their life jackets around their waists when they should have been up around their armpits. With 30-35lb packs on their backs they were just tipped upside down in the water and couldn't right themselves.

I can understand why the government kept it secret at the time because the news would have been a terrible blow to morale. I only question why it took so long for the facts to come out.'

Right: **Allied soldiers pause to inspect a French memorial to those who died in the carnage of World War I, before continuing with the liberation of western Europe.**

dropped at 2am into east and west flanks of the landings.

When they approached the beach, they saw what appeared to be men walking on water. These were crew members of the midget submarines used to guide in the flotillas of landing craft. Men lashed themselves to the masts of their tiny submarines, which floated low in the water to signal to the captains of much larger vessels.

H-HOUR, D-DAY

Just a few hours later, naval big guns were joining the aircraft in the pounding of enemy positions. Before 6am, the first men were ashore, putting months of rigorous training to the test.

British and Canadian troops were destined for the easterly beaches between Arromanches and Ouistreham. The three beaches earmarked for landings were code-named Gold, Juno and Sword.

In the west, the Americans tackled beaches Utah and Omaha, stretching between Les Dunes de Varreville and Colleville. On each of the beaches there were barbed-wire hazards, anti-tank stumps entrenched in the sand and other menaces. First to come off the boats were the commandos who were to knock out the pill-boxes, and the sappers, charged with clearing a safe path up the beach.

The operation surprised the Germans, who at first believed the landings to be a diversionary tactic. Rommel, in charge of defending the Atlantic Wall, was so unprepared for the Allied arrival that he was in Germany celebrating his wife's 50th birthday when the landings occurred. After Rommel heard of the invasion at 10.15am, he began a frantic drive back from Germany to his post. 'If I was commanding the Allied forces right now, I could win the war in fourteen days,' he confided to a colleague on his staff.

After the war, Rommel's son Manfred recalled how his father had told Hitler many times that the invasion battle could not be won. Hitler refused to listen. 'All my father could do was to pull the front further and further back and, until he was wounded, carry out his duty.'

When he was told of the early-morning events of 6 June, Hitler ordered his troops to clean up the beachheads before nightfall. He knew the only way to save his extended empire was to throw the Allies back into the sea. But convinced it was a false alarm, the Führer refused to release two Panzer divisions from the east of France to counter the Allied attack until 3.40pm.

The Führer refused to release two Panzer divisions from the east of France

Troops on Sword, Juno and Gold made solid progress in spite of casualties, although many soldiers landed without their guns and ammunition, which were lost in the water. They had to wait in huddles until the beach was taken before resuming their war. Blasting in their ears was the non-stop sound of the naval guns. On Utah beach, the German defences found it impossible to keep the swarms of Americans at bay. It was speedily taken with fewer than 200 lives lost.

HELL OF OMAHA

Unfortunately, on Omaha the poor weather combined with strong currents and fierce resistance to make the landings a hellish nightmare. Here the failure of the air forces to knock out large artillery was keenly felt. There was also the unexpected presence of a German division posted to Normandy on defensive exercises.

More than 2,000 men lost their lives. They were drowned when they were swept away by a changing tide with heavy equipment strapped to their backs. Some died when they trod on mines. Others perished from artillery, machine-gun, mortar and rifle fire from beach pill-boxes and from positions on cliffs above the beach. Wounded men strewn on the beach were in danger of being run over by tanks. There was little shelter and no escape.

◆ EYE WITNESS ◆

George Ross, from Glasgow, was called up in 1939 when he was 19 years old. He recalls how as sergeant major of 101 Company, 5th Beach Group, he landed on Sword beach in the early hours of D-Day.

‘We didn't know what we were going to come up against. The crossing was rough. Our craft was led by a chief petty officer. He had been at sea 25 years and never been sea-sick. But he was sick as a dog that morning.

Coming ashore, the first thing we noticed was a camouflaged pill-box. We got underneath the slits and launched a grenade attack. Our job was to establish a route where our tanks could come through. I honestly cannot say I was nervous. I was anxious but I had been warned about what to expect during six months of lectures beforehand.

There were bodies in the water of both British and Germans. One of the officers told us afterwards how, when he was walking up the beach, he felt he was walking on cushions. It was bodies of dead soldiers he was walking on.’

Lieutenant-General Omar Bradley considered a withdrawal. It would have been disastrous for the invasion, offering an opening for the Germans to attack both British and American flanks. Yet hardy US Rangers finally scaled the coastal heights to tackle the problem guns and alleviate the problems on the beach.

■ LONGEST DAY ■

Some of the men on the beaches were battle-hardened veterans. There was, however, a large contingent of raw soldiers, particularly among the Americans. They were pitched into the most intense, violent battleground, and forced to pick their way among the dead and dying amid the roar of big guns overhead and the sensation of small-arms fire whizzing past their ears. The air was filled with the pungent smell of flesh, blood and cordite.

Particularly on Omaha but also true of the other beaches, the first wave of men forced to fight their way ashore were cut down. Preparing to take to the beaches, the second wave witnessed the carnage then ran past the bodies of their comrades, hoping they didn't meet the same miserable fate.

Alongside panic there was determination – each flash of cowardice displayed by frightened, confused men was matched ten times by instances of heroism and stoicism. Minor troubles and petty differences lay forgotten. Each man was focused only on surviving for the next minute, the next hour and into the following day.

Ahead of them lay the task of capturing German-held towns, some of which fell more quickly than others. Russians who had been forced into German uniforms after being captured on the Eastern front were eager to lay down their arms. French people rushed out to greet the liberating Allies, offering drinks, flowers and greetings. A few French residents near the beaches braved the conflict to aid the wounded and dying.

Tales of outstanding courage filled the newspapers for months and years afterwards. One commando corporal led his men up the beach past enemy pill-boxes, bellowing encouragement. He fell only when he had passed the pill-boxes – he had received more than 50 wounds.

The defending Germans were mostly in chaos. One senior commander reported in panic that American gliders were landing Volkswagen cars in Normandy which were driven by American troops in German uniforms. Arguably, the day was as much lost by the confusion and indecision that paralysed many Germans as won by the heroic efforts of the Allied troops.

By the end of ‘the longest day’, 10,000 Allied soldiers had fallen. The figure was a third of that estimated by Allied command. But there was no turning back. The Allies had achieved the Normandy landings. Nothing and nobody was going to force them out of France again.

Below: A Sherman tank, affectionately nicknamed ‘Betty’, goes ashore to fight the battle of Normandy.

TANKS COME OF AGE

The tank came of age during World War II and proved to be a battle winner – or loser. The first tanks had been designed by Sir Ernest Swinton and saw action in the Somme offensive of World War I in 1916. Caterpillar tracks enabled them to cross treacherous terrain where no other vehicle could go. They were equipped with one or more guns, the crew sitting behind armour plating and firing off salvos at the enemy.

Now German general Heinz Guderian used the outbreak of World War II to put his own theories about the use of tanks to the test. Tanks should not be pinned down to flanking foot soldiers, he argued. Their purpose was to break out against the enemy, putting a speed into land-based warfare which it had never known before.

With that in mind, he formed his highly efficient Panzer divisions. The tanks were fast but lacked adequate protective armour. Nevertheless, they were an integral part of 'Blitzkrieg', the lightning war, a tactic with which Hitler easily won Poland, France, Holland and Belgium.

The technique took Britain and France by surprise. Although France had an enormous number of tanks at its disposal, 2,475 to be exact, their effectiveness was muted because of the old-fashioned way in which they were deployed. Instead of combining the firepower as Guderian did, each tank was evenly spaced down a long defensive line. In time Allied commanders mimicked Guderian to get the best out of their tanks. Used individually, they were easy targets.

When a tank 'brewed up', the escape hatches were wholly inadequate, or blocked

If tankmen in World War I were better protected than their colleagues in the infantry, the same could not be said of their counterparts 20 years on. In fact, there were few infantrymen who would willingly change places with tankmen. For while tanks stole a march on the enemy in the the killing fields of Flanders, technology had now caught up. Now there was a wide range of anti-armour artillery designed to knock tanks out. Men inside a stricken tank had little or no chance of escape.

And for the first three years of the war, German tanks and anti-tank weapons were appreciably better than their British counterparts. For example, the Mark II Matilda was known for its weak steering clutches, the Valentine offered only limited vision to its commander, the Crusader was mechanically unreliable. It took only an armour-piercing shell from one of the new breed of anti-tank guns used by the Germans to finish them.

That's when infantrymen remained heartily glad they had the job they did. For when a tank caught fire, or 'brewed up', the tiny escape hatches on the tanks were wholly inadequate and, in any case, were often blocked. Sometimes there was a matter of seconds before fire took a hold and the tank's ammunition began to explode. Sometimes there was not. Nicknames for tanks during the war included 'steel coffins', 'tommy cookers' and 'Ronson burners', because, like the products of the same name, they would always 'light first time'.

Above: **Tank crews during World War I were rightly delighted with the new hardware, which provided them with ample protection. But in World War II, a variety of anti-armour weapons existed to make life hell for the tankman.**
Far left: **The men of an armoured division running through the smoke-filled streets of the German town of Wernberg.**

BLACKENED DOLLS

One witness gruesomely detailed the effects on the men trapped inside: 'Little blackened dolls about two feet high have been found in tanks. Once these were men.'

As the war progressed, the Germans learned about the shortcomings of their tanks, which were

Left: **Matilda tanks were favoured by the British military but they failed to match the firepower of German Tigers, pictured below.**

A later generation of Allied tanks, including Shermans and Churchills, began to overcome some – but not all – of the difficulties. Yet no design, no matter how superior, could compensate for the problems thrown up by the terrain the tanks were working in. Every theatre of war offered its pitfalls to tanks. In Europe the rain made the earth unacceptably boggy; in North Africa the desert dust clogged engines and sharp stones tore the tracks; in Asia, where there were few tanks, the humidity affected the engineering. In nine days of fighting in Germany in 1945 the 9th Royal Tank Regiment and the 147th Regiment suffered 85 tank casualties – and only 17 were due to enemy action. No less than 36 succumbed to mechanical problems while 32 got stuck in the mud. Nevertheless, while tanks did much to speed the progress of Germans into France, they also helped to chase those same invaders

lacking in firepower and suffered from flimsy armour. Their most painful lesson came on the Eastern front when their troops encountered the fearsome T-34 tanks of the Russian armoured divisions.

Accordingly they introduced the Panther, in July 1943, and the Tiger, in September 1942, which were battle winners thanks to the enormous range of their guns, quite outstripping the British models, which were unable to get close enough to counter-attack effectively.

THE DEADLY 88

By the time the British developed the six-pounder gun, the Germans had in their armoury the heavier 75mm weapon. As the Americans caught up, with their own 75mm gun, the Germans leaped ahead again, fitting the deadly 88mm guns, which were originally designed as anti-aircraft guns but wreaked havoc when mounted on the Tiger tank.

As an illustration of the immense advantage kept in hand by the Germans in terms of tank technology, a single Tiger tank operating in Normandy knocked out 25 British tanks, 28 armoured vehicles and killed an additional 80 infantrymen.

It seemed as if the British had learned nothing from their experiences in the desert a full two years earlier. The poor state of British and American tank technology was little short of a scandal. It left Allied tank crews disheartened and reluctant, a malaise which never affected the Germans.

The poor state of Allied tank technology was little short of a scandal

out of France. This time the innovators were the British. A series of modified tanks were used to breach the beaches at Normandy. Witnesses reported that some German soldiers threw down their guns and ran at the sight of this bizarre new breed.

Behind them was Major-General Sir Percival Hobart. Like his brother-in-law Montgomery, Hobart was outspoken and did not suffer fools gladly. His forthright manner won him few friends at the War Office and by 1940 he was retired. It was only the personal intervention of Churchill which installed Hobart back in the fight against Hitler.

A series of modified tanks were used to breach the beaches at Normandy

HOBART'S FUNNIES

Mindful that Allied troops would encounter all manner of defences during the landings, his priority was to install tough armour to protect the troops. Then he looked at ways of tackling an amphibious landing, crossing a minefield, blasting a well-fortified pill-box and travelling with heavy vehicles across boggy ground.

To get hefty tanks ashore from landing craft, he came up with the Duplex Drive, an amphibious tank with propellers and a canvas skirt to protect it from the water. When the tank made it to the shore, the canvas was lowered.

An adaptation of the Churchill tank helped to combat the threat of minefields. On the front he installed a large rotating drum hung with heavyweight chains, turned by power from the engines. This 'Crab' would

ROMMEL – DESERT FOX

Erwin Rommel, courageous soldier and gifted leader of men, became known as the Desert Fox thanks to his cunning in North Africa.

The son of a teacher, Rommel joined the army from his home town of Württemberg as an officer cadet and proved his early promise during World War I. Between the wars he taught at Germany's military academies and authored a book about infantry strategies which was published in 1937.

When war broke out, Colonel Rommel was put in charge of the troops guarding Hitler. Frustrated with his behind-the-lines role, he seized the opportunity early in 1940 to command the 7th Panzer Division which he took into action in France before it was occupied, striking as far north as the Channel coast.

A year later he was put in charge of the German troops sent by Hitler to bail out the beleaguered Italians in North Africa. He shone in his new role, despite his misgivings about his wavering Italian allies. His impressive early victories won him the rank of field-marshal.

He was held in high esteem by his men for his initiative and bravery. In an example of his charismatic leadership, he once leapt from a car to address a division of men: 'There is an English Armoured Brigade getting ready to attack you from the north and in the south there is an English mixed force which is advancing. Take care that you are finished with the first before the second arrives!'

Yet he was all but ready to pull out his exhausted men when Hitler ordered a strike on Cairo in Egypt. Once again, he found remarkable success until his supply lines became hopelessly overstretched as he ventured further into British-held territory. Weakened by lack of essentials and wearied by months of fighting, he was finally defeated and pursued out of Africa.

In 1944 Rommel was ordered by Hitler to secure the French coastline against Allied invasion. Even though he was already convinced the war was unwinnable, he tackled the unenviable task with a deep professional pride. Yet he received little practical support from the Führer despite his warnings that all would be lost if the enemy penetrated the insubstantial coastal defences.

Although at heart he was non-political, Rommel was recruited by plotters who wanted Hitler replaced. The popular and realistic Rommel was their chosen leader. It is unlikely, however, that he knew about plans to assassinate the Führer for he was deeply opposed to killing for political ends.

In any event, an attack by British bombers put Rommel in hospital with serious injuries when the abortive coup took place. Hitler himself was reluctant to expose Rommel as part of the plot against him. He knew only too well that he was vulnerable to the grass-roots affection won by Rommel. So he dispatched two generals to see his reluctant adversary to offer a deal. Rommel and his family would escape the shame of public exposure if he would take poison and eliminate himself as a threat to Hitler. On 14 October 1944 Rommel did as his leader asked and was buried with full military honours.

Right: **Rommel (left) confers with a subordinate during the desert campaign.**

explode the hidden mines without causing damage to the tank or its crew and could beat a path up a beach for soldiers to follow.

Another anti-mine device was the 'Plough', a harrow attached to a tank which would uproot mines before

When SS troops captured the crew of a Crocodile, they would shoot them

they could do any damage. The 'Ark', a tank with four long beams at each corner, became a bridge to span small ravines and enable troops and armoured cars to cross.

Providing a roadway for troops and vehicles through soft ground became the job of the 'Bobbin' tank. It had a large, rolled, heavy-duty canvas roadway attached to its front. As the tank trundled along, it unfurled the roadway for following traffic. But perhaps the most fearsome of his designs was the 'Crocodile', another modified Churchill tank, this time designed to throw a scorching flame for 120 yards. Attached behind was its own fuel depot on wheels. Its effect on the enemy was instant. So feared was this flame-thrower that when SS troops captured the crew of a Crocodile, they would shoot them straightaway. Inappropriately, the stable of inventions was called 'Hobart's Funnies' – although they offered little to the enemy to smile about.

RIFLES AND GUNS

These were not the only technological advances that assisted the Allies. In just four years, the advances in gun capabilities had been enormous. When the war started, the Allied stock of rifles dated mostly from the previous world war or before. Bolt-action guns like this were slow and cumbersome to carry and use.

Now rifles were smaller and lighter than ever before and fired faster too. Rates of fire were up in machine guns as well. The British Bren could now dispense an astonishing 500 rounds a minute, the same as the US Browning. New mortars were light enough for infantrymen to carry with them into battle.

But just as these assisted the battle in one respect, they were a hindrance in another. The pack of equipment loaded onto the back of the infantryman was heavier than ever. Soldiers had to rely on good, old-fashioned mules in some cases to transport the guns to the top of high, hostile escarpments in rugged terrain.

Even then the pre-prepared defences installed by the enemy were strong enough to resist the firepower of such weapons. Only bombs would have a sufficiently devastating effect and that called for air support.

Left: **Versatile Jeeps were put through their paces in Normandy during the autumn of 1944. Medics even used these rugged, four-wheel-drive vehicles to transport the wounded.**

Left: **Allied soldiers in Burma used newer, more powerful weapons to get the better of their enemy.**

Given the firepower, the men made use of it, expending thousands of rounds of ammunition a day. The prospect of ammunition shortage, not to mention shortage of fuel for tanks and food for men, was a daunting one. As all armies discovered during World War II, a fighting force was only as good as its supply line.

In Burma the Chindits had an advantage over their Japanese enemy through the regular supplies dropped in by aircraft. In Europe and Africa, improving methods of amphibious landings allowed the trucks which were being turned out by the thousand in America to reach the battle fronts and replenish the men.

WILLYS JEEP

Transport had to be reliable and tough to be of any use. In 1940, the Jeep made its debut, its name derived from the full name first given it – general purpose (i.e. 'GP') vehicle. First constructed by the Willys Overland Company, this legendary creation had speed and agility and was an instant hit with the army. It could tackle even the roughest terrain and was useful for transporting troops, small arms and other light loads. It further helped to make horses redundant on the battlefield.

EYE WITNESS

Sydney Hartley suffered a badly injured leg when he was in the third of three tanks sent forward to pinpoint the whereabouts of the enemy during a battle in the Tunisian campaign. It was later amputated just above the knee. He was 28 years old.

I knew the dangers of crossing open ground on enemy territory but I clearly remember thinking that, with a bit of luck, we might again just get out of this unscathed with us being the last tank in a line of three.

After about 150 yards I heard the voice of the squadron leader come through my headphones. "Third troop, halt. Turn right and engage the enemy tanks." As we turned we realised we had run into a trap. Just coming into their final positions were two German tanks or self-propelled guns. We were all taken by surprise.

I knew this was the moment of truth, life or death. I quickly estimated the range, our big 75mm gun was loaded, I put the sights on the target and fired. It was impossible to follow the tracer bullet because the sun was lying just behind the target. Then it didn't matter as I saw the German tank's gun flash and a split second afterwards our world exploded. Everything suddenly went black and I felt what seemed like a red-hot poker against my right leg.

Flames were rising and I knew I had to get out quickly. I tried to pull myself out of the turret but at waist high I realised something was holding me back, because I was still wearing my headphones. Then I made a superhuman effort and flung myself the eight-foot drop to the ground. I knew something was terribly wrong with me. I heard this soul-destroying scream – it could have been any one of us. I dragged myself away. Looking at my right leg, the shock was more mental than physical. The armour-piercing shot had taken away half of my calf and broken up the calf bone. The foot was dangling from what flesh remained.

I took out a large field-dressing from my pocket and made a tourniquet. It looked like the driver and co-driver hadn't made it out of the tank. The next tank in line was burning although the crew got out safely. Mortar bombs were dropping all around. The troop corporal carried me to the rest of the men which was excruciatingly painful. I had morphine tablets but felt faint from blood loss. I didn't know which was most painful, my leg or the burns on my hands and face. The top skin of my hands peeled back like roller blinds. I had a very bumpy ride on a Bren-gun carrier back to the echelon alongside an injured German soldier and his friend.

I was laid out on a stretcher, looking up at the sky, when I saw a Messerschmitt 109 come into view. It appeared to be heading straight for me. He started machine-gunning us. It was the first of three aircraft attacks before I was put in the ambulance and driven away.

THE PACIFIC

Sweeping Japanese gains left the Allies with their work cut out, yet there was a grim resolve among them to push the invaders back. The rocky road to triumph over the extended empire of the Rising Sun began in New Guinea.

Japanese plans to take the unoccupied sector of New Guinea with a seaborne invasion were dashed following the Battle of the Coral Sea in May 1942. But they had not given up hope of seizing the island. Another offensive was planned, this time overland.

On 21 July 1942 an advance party of 2,000 Japanese soldiers landed at Buna, Papua, without a shot being fired. Their aim was to take Port Moresby, still in Allied hands. Ahead of them was a choice of two jungle tracks across the 1,200ft Owen Stanley mountains – hostile and steamy terrain. They chose the most accessible or least impassable.

Defensive forces on New Guinea at the time comprised some scattered Australian brigades backed up by a limited number of indigenous New Guinea riflemen.

The Japanese forces seized the interior in little more than a week, scaling the rocky heights of the mountain range. Racing against time, the Australians rushed through reinforcements. By 12 August Lieutenant-General F. Rowell, in command at Port Moresby, decided he had enough troops at his disposal to send an expedition into the mountains.

PORT MORESBY

Another Japanese force, numbering about 11,500, was landed, enabling a significant thrust to take place against the Australians. The prospects looked bleak for the Allies as the Australians fell back and back. The Australian commandos were swallowed up in the Japanese advances.

But by now the Japanese were encountering some difficulties of their own. Allied aircraft were making a fine job of disrupting the already treacherous lines of supply. It meant soldiers fighting in the most torrid conditions were left without adequate food and medical supplies.

In addition, the spectre of dysentry and other debilitating diseases loomed. Troops were weakened and finally killed by highly infectious wasting diseases which medics were unable to counter in jungle conditions. By September their advance had run out of steam. They were brought to a halt just 32 miles from Port Moresby.

Troops were weakened by highly infectious wasting diseases in jungle conditions

The Australians had little time to even draw breath. More Japanese troops had landed at Milne Bay, to the east, with orders to occupy the all-important airfield there. About 2,000 Japanese soldiers fought fiercely to reach the edge of the airstrip. Then the tide of battle turned against them. The Japanese had thought the Australian presence there was depleted. In fact there were nearly two brigades of men, two fighter squadrons and plenty of established artillery.

Above: **Japanese marines begin their march on New Guinea, confident of yet another victory.**

Left: **One of the Emperor's vessels lies wrecked off Guadalcanal, which became a graveyard for ships.**

In a counter-attack at the end of August by the 18th Australian Brigade, the Japanese were chased back to the sea. Finally, on 6 September, the remnants of the landing force were withdrawn.

Now the focus was back on the Japanese holed up in the mountain range. Australian troops reinforced by Americans forged up the Kokoda trail, the same route the invading Japanese had followed but in the opposite direction. A parallel force hoping to outflank the enemy embarked up the Kapa Kapa trail, even more remote and difficult.

Ahead of them lay the Japanese, securely dug into three defensive positions at the peak of the Kokoda trail. On 16 October the first Japanese post was taken by an Australian brigade. Yet the supreme effort in the face of determined opposition sapped what little strength the Australian soldiers had left.

Without the help of their Melanesian porters, who carried their equipment and sometimes the men themselves, they would not have got as far as they did. Try as they might, they could not budge the invaders from the other two dug-outs. Casualties mounted from sniper fire, with the Japanese apparently secure in their fox-holes.

The Australians were equally vulnerable to disease. The main cause of dysentry in New Guinea was polluted water. Springs were fouled by natives and the fighting men themselves, who were often too far away from their latrines to use them.

JAPANESE ROUT

It took fresh troops, who relieved the exhausted Australians, to add impetus to the assault. After intense fighting in swampy insect-ridden undergrowth the Japanese were finally routed. All the while, the Australian and American troops were benefiting from supplies dropped by air in the jungle. While some consignments went astray, the Allies were undoubtedly better off than their Japanese counterparts, who were still reliant on supplies coming in by sea and being passed up country. Australian troops found the bodies of their foe were emaciated and diseased. There were even signs of cannibalism as no doubt starving soldiers had resorted to eating human flesh to stay alive.

Every mile of the jungle between the heights of the mountains and the coastal plains was bitterly contested by the two sides. The stop-start campaign was at its most deadly when the Japanese were cornered in well-built defences, with their backs to the sea. Both prongs of the Allied forces joined up but there was stalemate as the Japanese sat tight in their well-dug positions.

Even the arrival of new Allied troops to wage the battle brought piecemeal results. For every fighting soldier, the conditions were nothing short of appalling. Climate and disease combined to make life barely tolerable. Allied troops were forced to pick off Japanese men and guns one by one as

EYE WITNESS

Bob Cartwright, from Wimbledon, south west London, was a lance corporal in the Royal Army Medical Corps who saw action in North Africa before being posted to the Far East. He served as a Chindit in the 44th Recce Regiment on the force's second foray.

There were 400 men in every column. The men from the medical corps like me travelled either at the front or the back. Conditions were ruddy awful.

The recce men had to tackle unmapped mountains with gradients of one in one. They were so steep that men had to crawl on their hands and knees. Even the mules fell by the wayside. They plunged down ravines and couldn't get out.

On my back was a 60lb first aid bag. For six weeks we were living on bully beef and biscuits and on any rice we could scrounge from local Burmese people, which wasn't much. Then US 'K' rations were air-dropped to us. In one of the daily meals there was usually a bar of chocolate. We used to melt it on to the rice to make a pudding.

We were on our way to Kohima to relieve the siege there when we were ambushed in a teak forest. The leaves of teak trees are very big and crisp. We had to wait until it rained before we could get out without the Japanese hearing our every footstep.

We had to take malaria and salt tablets. If you weren't wet from perspiration you were wet with the rain. Men suffered from malaria, tick bites and ulcers. I don't know anyone who didn't lose weight.

Everyone thought the world of Orde Wingate, the man behind the Chindits, even though he wasn't liked by the big shots in India. All they did was criticise him.

He had eyes that looked right through you and a really magnetic personality. I met him on two occasions. He inspired the troops.

We marched 600 miles through the jungle. I was out there about six months before they flew us out.

The men were in excellent spirits. I don't think I heard anybody moan about what we were doing. It was only the weather that bothered us.

There must be many unmarked and unknown graves in Burma.

Right: US soldiers take a well-deserved rest after action on New Guinea.
Below: Behind a screen of palms, the tanks of the US Marines rumble towards the Japanese front lines on Guadalcanal.

the doomed and diminishing force refused to capitulate. It wasn't until 3 January 1943 that the last of the Japanese resistance was ended. It had taken six months and cost an estimated 5,700 Australian, 2,800 American and 12,000 Japanese casualties.

As Australians and Americans fought to free Papua New Guinea, so US Marines were battling to liberate Guadalcanal, an island in the Solomons crucial in importance because of its airfield, Henderson Field. The conditions were equally squalid. Frequent rain squalls in the sauna heat made it a perfect breeding ground for mosquitoes. Malaria was rife among soldiers already weakened by the humidity. Nevertheless, both sides were doggedly determined that Guadalcanal should be theirs. Documents from Japan's high command captured later revealed the immense importance they attached to the island. 'Success or failure in recapturing Guadalcanal is the fork in the road which leads to victory for them or us.'

GUADALCANAL

On 7 August 1942 11,000 Marines were landed on Guadalcanal, surprisingly, without opposition. It would take a long time before Japan's soldiers on the island were eradicated, however. Japanese forces on neighbouring islands gave a more rousing reception to landing parties. On Tulagi, there was a hectic battle. At the end of it, the Marines were victorious. Tulagi was theirs. In total 108 US Marines had died while the Japanese force of an estimated 1,500 was wiped out.

Frequent rain squalls in the sauna heat made it a perfect breeding ground for mosquitoes

Like the Australians and the British, the American forces fighting the Japanese in the Pacific discovered that jungle warfare was a battle of nerves. The vegetation was host to scores of unusual animals making weird and terrifying noises. Sounds of birds, lizards and insects echoed through the night, each one sounding like an approaching sniper. And sometimes it was indeed the enemy, creeping stealthily in the dark before moving in for a kill. It was vital for guns to remain quiet unless there was an attack, since a burst of fire pinpointed a soldier's position for the enemy.

The Japanese, throughout the Pacific and South East Asia, displayed a mastery of cunning jungle warfare tactics. They knew a grenade thrown from somewhere in the night would result in havoc in an Allied camp. Startled and confused, the Allied soldiers would fire wildly and draw their knives, often injuring their comrades in the subsequent chaos. Meanwhile, the Japanese melted back into the darkness.

There were reports of Japanese soldiers leaping suddenly into Allied foxholes brandishing knives – then equally quickly jumping out again. The Allied soldiers were left tussling among themselves in panic with weapons drawn.

In the darkness, a voice might sound: 'Please, Johnny, help me.' It was tempting for the soldiers to rise up and respond to a call for help. If they did so, it would spell their doom. Here was yet another technique used by the Japanese to get the enemy to reveal itself.

The Japanese displayed a mastery of cunning jungle warfare tactics

The US occupation of Guadalcanal sparked some vital sea battles. But the first land-based reprisals from the Japanese came on 18 August when 1,000 Japanese troops were landed on Guadalcanal. All were killed and their commander Colonel Ichiki committed suicide.

Aircraft from the US carriers patrolling in the region deterred further large-scale landings although there were numerous small-scale attacks mounted by Japanese units, all successfully repulsed. Japanese commanders had grossly underestimated the number of American troops stationed on Guadalcanal. The American garrison, now numbering 19,000, was able to prevent wholesale Japanese landings with naval and air support even though the empire gathered 20,000 men from around the region for an October offensive.

The Americans were, however, handicapped by the frequent attacks on Henderson Field made by battleships and aircraft, as well as by the nuisance raids led by the Japanese who had successfully landed on

Below: **A tense moment as US soldiers, with guns at the ready, probe a jungle hideout in search of Japanese snipers.**

Guadalcanal. It wasn't until the three-day Battle of Guadalcanal at sea that the hard-pressed American defenders enjoyed some respite.

It was then that the Japanese navy decided to pull back from Guadalcanal and defend a different line. Senior navy commanders recognised the increasing strength of the Americans reduced the chances of taking Guadalcanal to virtually nil.

CHINDITS

The army was keen to continue the campaign, confident that the 30,000 troops it now had on the island would eventually overcome. But, without naval co-operation, there was no way of transporting further reinforcements to the island, or supplies to its troops.

Here was a chance at last for the Marines to withdraw for some recuperation after four months of jungle warfare. Their replacements finally totalled about 50,000 men, fit enough to drive the remaining Japanese forces from the island with relative ease. By February 1943, all had been evacuated by sea.

In Burma, the Japanese were still holding their own, having chased the British and Australian forces back to India. Yet the British were not left playing with an empty hand. They had one card left, which may not have been a winner but certainly kept them in the game. This was the first ever deployment of Long Range Penetration Groups, later known as the Chindits.

Behind the Chindits was Orde Wingate, an unorthodox soldier with broad experience of organising guerrilla operations. His men from the 77th Indian Brigade derived their name from the mythical Burmese temple guardian, the chinthe, half lion and half eagle.

Earlier in the war, Wingate had attempted suicide by stabbing himself in the neck while suffering from malaria and depression. He was saved and a year later brought his charismatic brand of leadership to an enthusiastic bunch of men.

Above: **B-25 Mitchell medium bombers of the US 5th Air Force deliver destruction to a Japanese airstrip on New Guinea in March 1944.**

INTO BURMA

Their aim was to operate behind enemy lines, causing disruption and damage wherever possible. That meant they had to be skilled jungle fighters with the qualities of the chameleon, able to fade away into the thickly forested landscape as quickly as possible. Those in demand for the first Chindit expedition in February 1943 were men who were masters of demolition skills and also able radio operators. The radio operators were vital to the success of the mission as they were responsible for contacting base and requesting supplies. These were dropped by air, giving the Chindits an essential advantage of endurance.

Together with elephants, mules and buffaloes, two groups compris-

◆ EYE WITNESS ◆

Bill Jenkins joined the Australian armed forces in 1939 when he was 18 years old and served until 1945, seeing action on the infamous Kokoda trail in New Guinea.

"We had just come back from the Middle East. I had three days' leave after two and a half years at war when I was recalled and put on a boat headed for New Guinea. Things were getting pretty desperate. The Japanese were in rowing distance of Australia itself. The pitifully small forces there to meet them were militiamen or home guard members who were decimated. We joined them and gradually drove the Japanese back over the Owen Stanley range of mountains. Sickness was terrible, with scrub typhoid, malaria and malnutrition claiming many lives. It was difficult for the planes to spot us and drop supplies. My brigade began with about 2,500 men. Less than 200 were evacuated at the close of the campaign. I returned weighing less than seven stones instead of 12 stones."

ing 3,200 men set off into occupied Burma, each ready to sub-divide into columns to achieve its aim. So well supplied were the men in the beginning that they even carried spare pairs of false teeth – as a man who could not eat, could not fight. They set off with the poetic words of Orde Wingate ringing in their ears:

WINGATE'S WORDS

'It is always a minority that occupies the front line. It is a still smaller minority that accepts with a good heart tasks like this that we have chosen to carry out. We need not, therefore, as we go forward into conflict, suspect ourselves of selfish or interested motives. We have all had the opportunity of withdrawing and we are here because we have chosen to be here; that is, we have chosen to bear the burden and heat of the day. Men who make this choice are above the average in courage. We need therefore have no fear for the staunchness and guts of our comrades.

'Our motive may be taken to be the desire to serve our day and generation in the way that seems nearest to our hand. The battle is not always to the strong nor the race to the swift. Victory in war cannot be counted upon but what can be counted upon is that we shall go forward determined to do what we can to bring this war to the end which we believe best for our friends and comrades in arms, without boastfulness or forgetting our duty, resolved to do the right so far as we can see the right.'

Wingate's bold and unexpected plan took the Japanese by surprise. When the forces crossing the main

EYE WITNESS

Alf Turner was a member of the 6th Battalion, The Devonshire Regiment, when he was posted to the Far East in 1943.

"Our sergeant major told us it was the best draft of all and that we wouldn't do anything for six months. That was a load of tripe.

After arriving at a reinforcement camp we were sent up to Bhopal to do a month's jungle training. Then we set off for Burma.

All you can see around you in the jungle are trees. If somebody fires, you don't know which way it is coming from. Being a country boy, I found it a bit easier than the Londoners out there who weren't used to night-time noises and wildlife.

The Japanese soldiers would shout out in the night: "Tommy, where are you?" And they would beat bamboo sticks to unnerve us. They tried to get us to give away our positions.

After one attack an apparently wounded Japanese soldier was calling: "Tommy, help me, help me." One of our officers who couldn't stick it any more went out to him. We told him not to go. When he got near, the soldier jumped up and threw a grenade at him. The officer lost his leg.

The Japanese put grenades under dead bodies in the hope you would turn them over.

Near the Irrawaddy river we came across a village where all the men had been beheaded by the Japanese and all the women were hung up by their hands and disembowelled. They were cruel fighters.

We took very few prisoners. Those who were wounded would rip their bandages off after being treated. They wanted to die in battle.

We belonged to the 20th Indian Division and I was a technical sergeant in charge of transport. I had to use sticky tape to repair tyres. We came across some Japanese supplies and used those to keep the trucks going.

There were giant ant hills. In the monsoon season they would collapse and you could find yourself knee deep in earth with ants crawling all over your legs. Then there were the leeches. The only way to get them off was with a lighted cigarette butt. We also had snakes slithering over our legs, jungle sores and prickly heat.

In France and Germany the troops had fleets of invasion craft. When they liberated towns, the people came out to cheer them. In Burma we had a few 'ducks' but mostly we had to make our own rafts to see us across the rivers. And we were never welcomed by the people. They didn't seem to care if it was us or the Japanese."

Left: **British troops of the 14th Army advance cautiously on the mud huts in the newly taken prize of Meiktila in Burma, March 1945.**

Irrawaddy and Chindwin rivers were spotted, commanders believed these were small groups on reconnaissance who would be easily dispatched. Only when major railway bridges were blown up did the Japanese suspect an orchestrated attack against them. At that stage, two divisions were sent to flush the British out of the jungle.

By now, the Chindits were dispersed into smaller, isolated groups, some faring better than others. That the Japanese were now aware of their presence made life increasingly difficult for the jungle warriors, who became trapped in the dense vegetation while their enemies had the run of the roads and tracks. Inevitably, the tightly planned operation began to fall apart. When food ran short, they ate their mules. But then they had no transport.

BAREFOOT TO INDIA

Four months later, some 2,200 men returned to India, hungry, physically frail and many with bare feet, veterans of a remarkable physical trial and fully conversant with both jungle and guerrilla tactics. True, they had proved little more than a mild hindrance to the Japanese. Yet important principles of warfare had been tried and tested by them, including that of air-dropping supplies. The soldiers rarely visited local villages for food and drink, where they might have been captured.

The Chindits were a difficult enemy for the Japanese to pin down, moving as they did under cover of darkness. So concerned were the Japanese army by the exploits of the Chindits that they revised their defensive policies in upper Burma, which not only tied up forces but ultimately laid them open to defeat.

Above: **Gurkha troops march past giant statues of chinthe – after which the Chindits were named – having liberated a key Burmese city.**

> ***That the Japanese were now aware of their presence made life increasingly difficult***

REICH IN RUINS

By the end of 1943, the Germans were on the run from Stalin's forces. The Battle of the Atlantic had ended in their defeat and U-boats were being systematically blown out of the water. Germany itself was suffering a barrage of bombing campaigns, Italy had changed sides and, to many in the Nazi hierarchy, it seemed the war was already lost.

The following year brought little by way of relief. The long-awaited landings of thousands of Allied soldiers finally occurred in Normandy in June. When German soldiers were unable to defend the beaches, it was clear the destination for the Allies was nothing short of the German Fatherland itself.

During their first few weeks on French soil, the Allied armies encountered some strong resistance, particularly centred at Caen. Here was a professional SS division and a green German unit culled from the Hitler youth. Although some fighters were as young as 16, they were fired with enthusiasm and proved to be formidable opponents.

The British forces failed to capitalise on their surprise attack to gain their D-Day objectives and paid the penalty for their short delay while regrouping, as the Germans dug in with a vengeance. It took two major pushes, code-named 'Epsom' and 'Goodwood', to oust the few hundred Germans in residence, costing hundreds of Allied lives.

Countless numbers of French civilians died, mostly in the enormous air raids launched by the Allies which reduced the historic town of Caen to rubble. Fires raged in Caen for 11 days after the main bombing attack. Estimates put the number of French dead as high as 10,000. Still the German resistance held fast. The net effect of the air raids was simply to provide new hazards, like blocked roads, for the Allied ground forces.

TANK BATTLES

There were bitter tank battles between the newly landed British and Canadian forces and the Panzer units which rushed to the area from eastern France and Poland. Supplies began to falter when a gale blew up in the Channel on 19 June, wrecking the Mulberry harbours, onto which the Allies were unloading.

Churchill and the American leaders were filled with angry frustration. There was talk of sacking Montgomery for his failure to move forward. But while German reserves were embroiled in the battle, other Allied divisions were given a free hand elsewhere on the coast.

The Americans were making more headway. Having captured the Cherbourg peninsula, troops broke out to make a sweep through central Normandy. US troops discovered too the horrors of fighting in the Normandy bocages. This was the ancient hedgerow and field system covering the countryside providing havens for German snipers and hazards for Allied tanks and infantrymen.

Churchill and the American leaders were filled with angry frustration

The German reinforcements, which had at last made their way to Normandy, created more firmly held pockets of resistance, which were tough to shift. Falaise, Metz and a number of other towns formed serious blockages in the arteries of the Allied invasion.

Soldiers who on D-Day had never fired a shot in anger or seen a dead body were within a matter of weeks brutalised by the harshness of conflict. If they were fearful, they hid their feelings. Many were overwhelmed with elation when they killed an enemy soldier. As one US Ranger explained: 'It was not joy that I had killed him but that he hadn't killed me.'

Far left: **French inhabitants and US soldiers rejoice after Cherbourg is won from the Germans.**

Left: **German soldiers surrender to the US military near Toulon, in southern France, following the invasion of the south of the country in August 1944.**

By 15 August 1944 the Germans found southern France was also at risk. 'Operation Dragoon' got underway 10 weeks after D-Day, with the forces of the US 7th Army making landings between Toulon and Cannes and meeting only mild opposition.

The advance through France was known as the 'Champagne Campaign'

Among the soldiers to land at the beaches south of St Tropez was a 20-year-old Audie Murphy, later to be a Hollywood hearthrob, who single-handedly wiped out an enemy machine-gun nest.

The US forces drove up France, keen to link up with their comrades swinging down from the north. Such was the ease of the advance, and the joy of their reception by the French, it became known as the 'Champagne Campaign'. Paris was liberated by Free French forces on 25 August.

ARNHEM

By September, Montgomery and American general Omar Bradley had thrust through Belgium and Luxembourg. The fighting remained gruelling with British paratroops experiencing horrific losses when they tried to take Arnhem, Holland, at the end of September.

Finally, the successes of the Allies began to take their toll. The front line forces were running out of ammunition and other supplies while enemy soldiers were making stronger

EYE WITNESS

Rudolf Valentin was among the German soldiers who fought at Monte Cassino, and revealed some of his experiences to New Zealand author Alex Borrie. He saw some tough fighting as the Germans tried to recapture Hangman's Hill.

Our situation was not an enviable one. Whoever came out of cover during the day became a sure victim for the Indian sharp-shooter. The Gurkhas on Hangman's Hill were in a similar position. They also had to make themselves scarce during the day otherwise they drew German fire.

The set of circumstances meant that almost all attacks were switched to night-time. Just after the onset of darkness, we had to repel the first attack and two others followed. With the beginning of the new day, we had to creep into holes again which we enlarged with the spikes of our jack-knives. We had to survive the armed attacks in these holes.

In the evening the murderous close-combat began again. During this one often had to let the enemy advance until only metres away before one was able to recognise him by the shape of his helmet. In addition to this, hunger and especially thirst were also becoming factors.

At dawn on 19 March the 1st/FJR 4 [a German paratroop unit] came out to us with about 120 men from the monastery with the order to capture Rocca Janula again. After approximately 10 minutes of machine-gun fire and shelling our comrades overwhelmed the Rajputanis at the lower hair-pin curve and stormed the walls.

A terrible hand-to-hand combat flared up there. The Germans were attempting to scale the walls. They succeeded in blasting a hole in the wall. But the enemy from the Essex Battalion fought with the same determination and beat off the attack causing heavy casualties. Courage and the willingness to make sacrifices did not help at all. The castle could no longer be captured. This attack cost the lives of half the comrades, the rest had to retreat.

But the English and the Indians also suffered such heavy casualties that they had to abandon their intentions to capture the monastery in this way. On this day a ceasefire lasting several hours was agreed upon in order to recover the dead and wounded. It was at this point that we exchanged cigarettes with the enemy and helped each other out with bandages. The English even lent us stretchers to transport our wounded to the monastery. At the same time the Gurkhas took their wounded through our positions. A short time later the men who helped each other out in such a comradely fashion were once again the bitterest of enemies. What madness!

Right: **Although General de Gaulle was never popular among Allied war leaders, he won the undying adoration of his people for his uncompromising views.**

Right: **German soldiers came uncomfortably close to succeeding in their objective of reaching the Belgian port of Antwerp during the Battle of the Bulge.**

stands than before. Waiting for relief, the Allied initiative ground to a halt in December 1944 before going on to make headway in Germany.

The infantrymen were heartily relieved. It had been a long, arduous haul which cost many lives. Combat exhaustion as well as other maladies were striking the servicemen who had survived the fighting. Seemingly ceaseless rain and acres of mud weighed their spirits down.

SLOW ADVANCE

Many soldiers were weary of the inch-by-inch advance they had experienced in some of the fiercest battles waged on the Western front, which resembled the trench warfare known by their fathers two decades earlier. A rash of self-inflicted wounds began bringing waves of soldiers to the sick bays. Anyone who was suspected of having deliberately injured himself was instantly court martialled.

Their commanders, meanwhile, were frustrated in their desire to push relentlessly onwards. Hitler seized the

The fury of the American and British air forces was brought to bear on the Germans

opportunity to strike back. Choosing the same route which had served him so well some four years earlier, he proposed a surprise attack through the Ardennes with the intention of driving a wedge between the Allied forces and capturing Antwerp, the Belgian port through which vital Allied supplies were being brought.

Luck was with the Germans as the bold offensive got underway on 16 December. Low cloud was keeping the Anglo-American reconnaissance aircraft on the ground. The Allied commanders had no idea of what was coming until it arrived.

Field-Marshal von Rundstedt commanded the German forces, comprising ten armoured divisions and 14 other divisions. However, only the 6th SS Panzer Army was up to full strength and adequately equipped. When the weather cleared, the fury of the American and British air forces was brought to bear on the Germans. Fighting raged on over Christmas and into the New Year, with the Allies gradually gaining the upper hand. The Battle of the Bulge, as it was called, was over by 23 January when the Allies took St Vith, the last remaining German stronghold. Another, less substantial German thrust into northern Alsace which began on 1 January 1945 was also quickly suppressed.

The cost of the two German assaults was high. Both had weakened the German defences elsewhere, a fact that didn't go unnnoticed by Allied commander General Patton. At last the fortified Siegfried line, built to protect Germany, was in danger.

February saw a further big offensive in north west Europe from the Allies. In a series of pushes the Allied armies managed to link up to form a formidable front line.

REMAGEN

They were bucked when a sharp-eyed US sergeant spotted a railway bridge left intact by the retreating Germans, spanning the Rhine at Remagen. The Germans had viewed the Rhine in much the same way as the English saw the Channel, a vital line of defence which would be hard to penetrate. Now troops forged along the bridge while further up- and downstream their comrades made less comfortable crossings on swiftly assembled pontoons. The defences of the Fatherland had been breached.

EYE WITNESS

LeRoy Stein, from Michigan, USA, was 24 when he joined up and was a member of the 87th Division in Patton's 3rd Army in the battle for Normandy.

'It was very frightening. I was in a mine platoon which was shaky work. We laid mines and booby traps and would take them up if they had no more use. Each one was supposed to be removed. A permanent record was supposed to be kept on the whereabouts of these explosives. But they were not properly taken up. There are still people being killed by them today.'

Airborne troops landed on a large scale helped capture stalwart German towns. By early May, key regions including the Ruhr, Hamburg, Bavaria and Austria were in the hands of the Allies. Yet the battles had been grim. The German defences were cleverly conceived and included mines and booby traps.

Frequently, the morale of troops was low. In addition to seeing bloody action and burying their friends, the infantry had to endure apparently endless hours of foot-slogging. Their rations were pitiful, consisting mostly of tinned spam, corned beef and soya sausages. Despite the strong camaraderie of men forced to suffer unspeakable hardships, there were numerous instances of insubordination and desertion in the field.

Meanwhile, Russian troops had been pouring into Germany from the east, their target Berlin. Even the most hopeful of German commanders must have realised the end was near when a tidal wave of Russian troops overran the Silesian industrial basin in January. Albert Speer, head of war production, wrote a memo to Hitler, beginning with the words: 'The war is lost.' Speer realised that Germany could not sustain its industry or defence when the region which produced 60 per cent of its coal had been snatched from it. But Hitler refused to listen.

RED FLAG RISES

Russian generals Zhukov and Konev encircled Berlin by 25 April and began another relentless advance towards the very heart of the Reich. Fierce street fighting raged as loyal Nazis battled to stop the Russians closing in on their beloved Führer. Loyal members of the Hitler Youth aged 12 to 14 joined in. Despite their efforts, a Red Flag was raised over the Reichstag on 2 May 1945.

As for Hitler, he finally summoned his long-time mistress Eva Braun to be at his side in the middle of April, realising that his days were numbered.

His 56th birthday on 20 April was marked by more catastrophes in the field. Nazis including Goebbels, Göring, Himmler, Ribbentrop and Bormann joined him for the muted celebrations. They urged him to flee south but Hitler refused to leave Berlin. In fact, he rarely left the 18-room bunker beneath Berlin's Chancellery that had become his home. With him were the commanders who had remained close to him, and his most valued aides.

He slept for no more than three hours at a time, partly as a result of the pounding of the incessant air raids. Incredibly, Hitler still talked of inflicting defeat on the Allies. The next day he ordered a last-ditch stand

Albert Speer, head of war production, wrote a memo to Hitler beginning with the words: 'The war is lost'

against the Russians, bellowing that every last man should be thrown in. The counter-offensive never had a chance to get off the ground.

When Hitler finally realised there was no hope, he erupted in a volcanic fury, accusing all his closest commanders of cowardice and treachery. For the first time he spoke of killing himself. Still, he refused to abandon

Right: **US army engineers attempt to put rails across the bridge at Remagen. Four hours after the picture was taken, the bridge collapsed into the Rhine.**

Above: **Soldiers of the US 9th Army flush out German soldiers in a battle-scarred town over Germany's western border. Meanwhile Russian troops bore down on Berlin from the east.**

the war effort, a stand which cost the lives of countless German soldiers left fighting against atrocious odds around Germany.

Inside the bunker the nervous exhaustion and psychological tension among its occupants reached new heights. Although he was sometimes calm, Hitler exploded in rage when he heard that his hitherto faithful lieutenants Göring and Himmler were both making advances to the Allies for peace.

On 27 April, Hitler carried out a macabre rehearsal of his suicide and the deaths of the faithful still at his side. However, it wasn't until 29 April that he dictated his will to his secretary. There was no expression of remorse for the misery and death he had caused worldwide, only the same tired tirade against those he held responsible for his misfortunes: 'More than thirty years have now passed since in 1914 I made my modest contribution as a volunteer in the First World War which was forced upon the Reich. In these three decades I have been actuated solely by love and loyalty to my people . . .

'It is untrue that I, or anyone else in Germany, wanted the war in 1939. It was desired and instigated solely by those international statesmen who were either of Jewish descent or who worked for Jewish interests.'

The last paragraph in Hitler's will read: 'Above all I charge the leaders of the nation and those under them to scrupulous observance of the laws of race and to merciless opposition to the universal poisoner of all peoples, international Jewry.'

HITLER'S END

In the early hours of the same day, Hitler married Eva Braun and had a champagne celebration with Bormann, Goebbels, his secretaries and his cook. Within hours he heard of the death of Mussolini, shot with his mistress Clara Petacci and then hung by the ankles in a square in the centre of Milan.

On the afternoon of 30 April, with the Russians just a street away, Hitler said his final farewells, retired to a sitting room with his wife and shot himself. Eva chose to end her life by taking poison.

The instructions he left for the disposal of his body were carried out, with his remains being burned by petrol fire in the yard of the bunker. With Hitler turned to ashes, his successor as Führer, Grand Admiral

◆ EYE WITNESS ◆

A diary recovered from a German soldier killed in the Allied push from Normandy contained these words.

It's Sunday. My God, today is Sunday. With dawn the edge of our forest received a barrage. The earth trembles. The concussion takes our breath. Two wounded are brought to my hole, one with both hands shot off. I am considering whether to cut off the rest of the arm. I'll leave it on. How brave these two are. I hope to God that all this is not in vain. To our left, machine guns begin to chatter ...

In broad waves you can see him across the field. Tanks all around him are firing wildly. Now the American artillery ceases and the tank guns are firing like mad. I can't stick my head out of the hole – finally, here are three German assault guns. With a few shots, we can see several tanks burning once again. The infantry take cover and the attack slows down. It's stopped. It's unbelievable that with this handful of men we hold out against such attacks.

Karl Dönitz, commander in chief of the German navy, tried to negotiate a peace settlement, but the Allies were unimpressed. They wanted nothing short of an unconditional surrender. And so, as pockets of German resistance capitulated around the former Reich, the surrender was finally signed on 7 May 1945.

BLACK SANDS OF IWO JIMA

America's mighty war machine was now in top gear. In the field the US had the latest and the best military equipment. At home its colossal industrial muscle provided seemingly endless supplies of hardware. There were ranks of young men drawn from all over the States queuing up for action, full of grit and determination.

In opposition, an over-extended Japan was war-weary. The country's battle losses in ships and planes far outstripped the number of replacements being produced on the home islands. Japan itself was being starved of the materials it desperately needed by the naval blockade imposed by America. Its industry was targeted for devastating air raids. Long-term jungle fighting had taken its toll among the surviving troops, despite their rigorous training.

Yet still the Japanese soldiers were threatening and tenacious. Against all odds, they were determined to hold back the American advance. In-bred in the Emperor's men was an oriental code of honour which dictated that they must fight to the death. In most cases, this is just what they did, costing many Allied lives. The hallmark of the Pacific campaign was prolonged savage fighting and huge loss of life.

The hallmark of the Pacific campaign was prolonged savage fighting and huge loss of life

With a victory established in New Guinea by the start of 1943, Allied commander of the South West Pacific General Douglas MacArthur was already pondering his route to the Philippines, a campaign dear to his heart. Before he could take it, there were a selection of Japanese strongholds on New Guinea still to be beaten.

Meanwhile, Admiral Halsey, of the South Pacific sector, already had the Russell Islands, Vella Lavella and Bougainville in the Solomon Islands under his belt.

Both MacArthur and Halsey recognised the value of leap-frogging many Japanese-held islands and outposts, picking for attack mainly those that were inadequately defended. The rest were left to 'wither on the vine', increasingly isolated from Japanese lines of communication.

Right: **Admiral William Halsey, commander of the 3rd Fleet, sits deep in thought on the bridge of the USS *New Jersey* en route for the Philippines.**

TARAWA

Now nine crucial atolls under Japanese control, collectively known as the Marshall Islands, had to be taken. A taste of the fierce fighting to come occurred on one of them, Tarawa, defended by 5,000 Japanese. When a similar number of US Marines landed on the island on 21 November 1943 they found themselves pinned down on the open beach. Before night had fallen, 500 of the Americans were dead and a further 1,000 wounded. Japanese gun positions were only silenced when their entire crew was killed. Only an additional landing of

Left: **General MacArthur remained determined to push the Japanese out of the Pacific. *Right:* An island beach devastated by gunfire becomes a depot for US troops.**

troops won victory for the Americans. In all 1,000 Marines died along with virtually all the Japanese.

The Americans learned a valuable lesson. When it came to taking another atoll in the group, Kwajalein, there were no landings until a heavy bombardment neutralised much of the defence.

Fleas, flies, lice and mosquitoes were liable to be carrying appalling disease

Although the American campaign was fast, there was immense hardship for the troops brought about by the conditions. Fleas, flies, lice and mosquitoes plagued them. More than just pests, they were liable to be carrying appalling disease. It wasn't until 1944 that DDT sprays were introduced to combat the insect swarms.

Once an island was taken, it became a top priority to bury the dead on both sides. For the corpses attracted not only flies but also rats, which came in droves.

MARIANAS

Truk, a key naval outpost for the Japanese navy, came under fire on 18 February 1944 in a raid orchestrated by Vice-Admiral Marc Mitscher. There were 30 separate strikes at the base which destroyed 275 aircraft and 39 ships.

Next stop was Saipan in the Mariana Islands, a fearsome task given that 32,000 Japanese soldiers were garrisoned there. Nevertheless, it was a dual disaster for the Japanese. For soon after the American landings on 15 June came the Battle of the Philippine Sea, in which their Fleet Naval Air Arm was decimated.

EYE WITNESS

Ito Masashi spent 16 years in hiding in the jungle of Guam after it was overrun. He describes his reason for not surrendering in his book *The Emperor's Last Soldiers*.

"By the start of October the only sound we heard was the shell fire so far off that it sounded like distant thunder. But the fighting continued. The enemy no doubt considered it simply mopping up but for us it was a full-scale and bloody battle.

We had eaten what little there was of our portable battle rations of dried bread and now we lived on what berries and fruits we could find. We kept up a vain defiance with nothing left to help us but our grenades. But now the vital will to fight was absent. Our commanders sent messages advising us to end the senseless resistance, to give up our arms and pack it in. But somehow we didn't. We were afraid to.

Afraid that our useless rifles and guns – marked with the noble crest of the Imperial Chrysanthemum – might fall into enemy hands, we buried them deep in the ground. And we prepared, quite resignedly, for death as the only possible outcome. For us soldiers of Japan, the only thing left to our way of thinking was to deck out our last moment as nobly and bravely as we could.

By now there was no supply base for us to go back to and we didn't know whether there still existed any company or battalion headquarters where we could have got orders. So we formed sad and sorry little squads, hardly alive, now hiding ourselves away in the jungle, now moving aimlessly along the paths and lanes. We had been reduced to the status of a ragged band of stragglers. Even during this period however there were a number of incidents when we tangled with Australian troops backed by tanks or fell foul of a line of pickets. Fortunately, we always managed to get in our grenades and escape. But on every occasion the number of our already small band would dwindle by the odd one or two."

And by July the defenders of Saipan were running short of ammunition. They chose to kill themselves by the score, along with the 22,000 civilians who had been living on the island since before the war, when it was a Japanese dominion. American troops looked on helplessly as women and children joined their menfolk in plunging from

high cliffs to be dashed on the rocks below rather than face the ultimate shame of surrender. Saipan was under US control by 9 July.

The islands of Tinian and Guam were the next to go. Then the Palau group of islands. Although it didn't take nearly as long to achieve victory here as it had done on Saipan, the fighting was every bit as ferocious. It frequently included suicidal rushes at secure American positions by shrieking Japanese soldiers, who were duly mowed down in their masses. With fighters refusing to surrender in even the most hopeless of battles, the Americans were forced to use armoured flame-throwers to clear well-protected pockets of resistance.

By October 1944 the Americans were ready to redeem the Philippines. The island of Leyte was their chosen point for invasion, poorly defended by just 16,000 men. While a memorable victory was quickly carved out for the Americans at sea, the land-based struggle for supremacy lasted longer, with the Japanese counter-attacking in December. The losses on both sides were heavy. The Americans mourned 15,500 fighters, while the Japanese suffered the body-blow of 70,000 deaths. Yet once Leyte was won for the Americans, the rest of the Philippines fell to them with gratifying ease.

At Iwo Jima the US Marines were cut down in droves by the defenders

Now it was time to approach the Japanese home islands. Choosing to by-pass several strongholds, including Formosa, the Americans decided to take the Ryuku Islands, less than 400 miles from Japan itself. A stepping-stone island between the Philippines and the Ryukus was deemed necessary as a rendezvous for American planes. Iwo Jima in the Bonin Islands was selected for invasion in February, while an operation to capture Okinawa, the largest of the Ryuku Islands, was timetabled for April.

Above: US Marines hold their weapons aloft as they wade ashore on the stepping-stone island of Tinian, unsure about what awaits them beyond the beach.

At Iwo Jima the US Marines were cut down in droves as they tried to penetrate the complex defensive system constructed by the defenders. Bombardment by battleship prior to the landings had not obliterated the defences as hoped. In fact, the Japanese were so deeply entrenched it had made little noticeable difference.

Amphibious landing transports were beached and blown up and the Marines found themselves without an iota of cover on their route up the

'FRIENDLY FIRE'

'Friendly fire' took its toll during World War II, particularly during the Normandy campaign.

Bombers had failed to dislodge German gun emplacements before D-Day. This should have acted as a warning against so-called precision bombing. Yet American heavy bombers were called on in July 1944 to target the German lines. Instead, the bombs fell on US troops, killing 25 and wounding 131. The next day, the same mistake was made again, only this time 111 American servicemen were killed and 490 were wounded. Among the dead was US Lieutenant-General Lesley McNair, the highest-ranking Allied officer to be killed in the Normandy campaign.

Three weeks later, 'friendly fire' claimed more Allied victims from above. This time 77 Canadians and 72 Polish soldiers died. 'Friendly fire' incidents occurred through poor weather conditions, imprecise briefings, lack of training and sometimes through nervous fingers being on the trigger.

beach. There was also little opportunity to remove the wounded from the firing line.

Japanese commander Lieutenant-General Kuribayashi's order to his men was acidly clear: 'No man must die until he has killed ten of the enemy.' He added that each of his men must think of his defence position as his graveyard. It was widely considered to be the worst landing the Marines experienced in the war. Iwo Jima finally fell into American hands on 16 March after they had used bulldozers to bury defenders in their bunkers. The tally of dead among the Americans amounted to 6,821 but yet again there was a far more devastating number for Japan as virtually all the 21,000 troops were killed.

On 1 April the landings by the Marines on Okinawa, as part of 'Operation Iceberg', were in stark contrast to the blood-bathed beaches of Iwo Jima. An estimated 50,000 Americans got ashore barely hearing a shot and for the following five days there was hardly a skirmish. It was a deliberate lull engineered by the Japanese before they unleashed a storm of incredible violence.

The Japanese had drawn up a defence plan code-named 'Ten-Ichigo', which involved thousands of 'kamikaze' missions. The Japanese commanders were even prepared to sacrifice their prized battleship Yamato in a suicidal attack. On 6 April the ship left its base with sufficient fuel for a one-way journey to Okinawa. Its aim was to wreak havoc there among the landing forces.

KAMIKAZE

However, soon picked up on radar, the great warship came under fire from 280 US aircraft until she was finally crippled and sunk on 7 April with her 2,300 crew still aboard.

Meanwhile, swarms of kamikazes were setting about the US Navy as it cruised off Okinawa. On the first day, three destroyers, two ammunition ships and an LST (Landing Ship Tank) were destroyed. It temporarily halted the drive forward, through lack of ammunition. On the next day a battleship, a carrier and two destroyers were hit. Of the 16 destroyers sent forward to give early warning of kamikaze raids, 14 were sunk before the end of the campaign even though they were of minimal stragetic value. The story goes that one destroyer's crew erected a poster complete with arrow bearing the words: 'To Jap Suiciders.

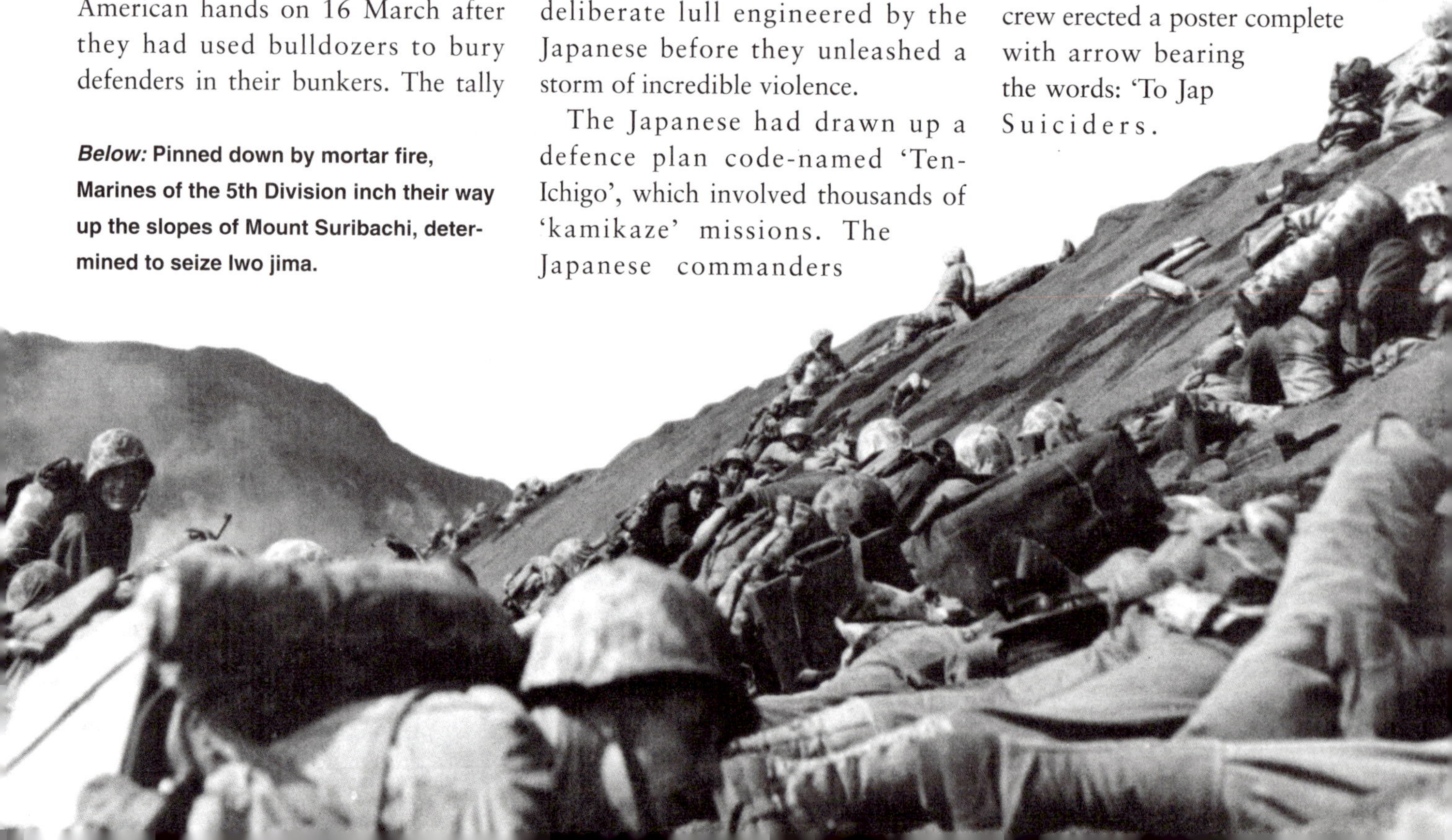

Below: **Pinned down by mortar fire, Marines of the 5th Division inch their way up the slopes of Mount Suribachi, determined to seize Iwo jima.**

Right: **On Okinawa, advancing Americans were forced to use fire power to oust tough Japanese resistance.**

Carriers are that way.' And still kamikaze fliers descended on the fleet.

During the battle to secure Okinawa, which raged between April and August, there were an estimated 2,000 kamikaze raids carried out by both army and navy aircraft as well as about 5,000 conventional sorties. In total 20 ships were sunk by kamikazes, often under a barrage of attacks by suicide pilots, against six sunk by other aircraft manoeuvres. Kamikaze planes notched up a further 217 strikes against ships.

Yet inevitably the Japanese resources were wilting under the strain. After two months of sustained kamikaze raids, there were few aircraft left for such missions.

On land the fighting was equally horrific. In one of the early battles, to win the off-island of Ie Shima and its landing strip, more than 4,700 of the 5,000 Japanese defenders died in battle. Towards the end of the eight-day confrontation, local women, some with babies strapped to their backs, draped demolition charges around their necks and rushed at American positions.

It took until the last days of June to eradicate the last of the Japanese land-based resistance on Okinawa. Total American losses amounted to almost 7,000 men as well as numerous ships and 763 planes. Unusually, the Americans found themselves taking prisoners, some 7,400 in all. Many of these were too sick or severely wounded to kill themselves. Meanwhile, 110,000 died in battle, with all the senior officers committing ritual suicide in their offices, and there was carnage among the population. The Japanese stood the loss of 7,800 aircraft.

After two months of sustained kamikaze raids, there were few aircraft left

The hostilites in South East Asia were just as gruesome for the troops involved. Following the Chindit offensive into Burma and a second, unsuccessful, attempt by the British to re-enter Burma at Arakan, the Japanese commander in Burma, General Renya Mutaguchi, decided that going on the attack against the British in India was probably the best form of defence.

On 6 March 1944 the 'U-Go' offensive opened, with three Japanese divisions setting off for Kohima and

Left: **Billowing smoke marks the path of a kamikaze plane which caused devastation on the USS *Bunker Hill*, hit off Okinawa on 11 May 1945.**

Imphal, high in the Assam hills. For the first time in the conflict, British troops stood firm against Japanese aggression in defence of India.

KOHIMA

Both Kohima and Imphal were under siege by the first week in April. There followed some of the harshest fighting of the war.

Japanese soldiers were in the majority but the Commonwealth troops were in no mood to be routed this time. The bitterest of the fighting was at Kohima. Japanese soldiers had killed everything in their path until they reached the tennis court of what was once the Deputy Commissioner's bungalow. They dug in on one side while the defenders were holed up just 20 yards away.

Grenades and mortar bombs rained down on the Commonwealth forces, taking a toll on the troops. However, they repelled the frequent Japanese charges with surprising ease. Each one was accompanied by the traditional 'banzai' cry and screaming. The Allies were able to open fire and cut them down. There was little opportunity for the Allies to collect their dead. Bodies lay rotting on the ground, emitting a terrible stench. Sometimes they were buried where they had fallen, in shallow, inadequate graves, with arms or knees left exposed. A cloud heavy with the pungent smell of burning flesh hung over the Allied position as the Japanese cremated fallen comrades.

Both sides were racked with tiredness and riddled with disease

Both sides were racked with tiredness and riddled with disease. Any minor abrasion could quickly become life-threatening through septicaemia and gangrene. After 16 days of gruelling fighting the defending regiments were relieved by the 1st Royal Berkshire Regiment.

They left behind 1,419 dead, among them 19-year-old Lance Corporal John Harman – born and bred on the tranquil island of Lundy – a strapping soldier who ran up to a Japanese machine gun, shot the crew and hoisted it up on to his shoulders to bring it back behind his own lines.

Further, he stormed a bakery held by the Japanese, set it on fire and came back to his dug-out with a wounded Japanese soldier under each arm. It was as he was returning from one of these astonishing feats that he was fatally wounded. He was awarded the Victoria Cross posthumously for his incredible efforts.

Airlifts by the American air force and RAF continued to aid the defenders of Kohima and Imphal. The Japanese soldiers had pitiful rations by comparison. It was a staggering 80 days before the Japanese were compelled to withdraw, with just a quarter of the original force left on their feet. Over half the casualties were claimed by sickness.

Above: **After a siege by the Japanese, the British 14th Army was finally able to open the Imphal-Kohima road.**